Why We Do Missions

To Avery

my Perspectives

classmate

John Lindner

May 10, 2022

WHY WE DO MISSIONS

Gripping stories show the transformation native missionaries bring to their neighbors, communities and nations.

BY JOHN LINDNER & ASSOCIATES

Photos are supplied from the leaders and ministries they illustrate.

An eBook version titled *Eight Transformed Lives; True Stories of God's Grace*, is available containing the short stories only.

To assist or obtain more information on any of the ministries mentioned in this book, please contact Advancing Native Missions via its website.

Copyright © 2022 by Advancing Native Missions
P.O. Box 29, Afton, VA 22920
www.advancingnativemissions.com

ISBN: 978-1-946174-17-8

Contents

Foreword

I have had the honor and the pleasure to work with John Lindner for 35 years. He is a great friend, beloved mentor and a walking role model of authentic Christianity. He has been writing about indigenous missionaries for 40 years and tells from the heart their tears and successes with authenticity. He loves them.

It was during my tenure as ANM President that I asked John to start a magazine for ANM with him as editor. In the ensuing years, with his consistent fervor for missionary stories and fierce observance of high standards of writing, editing and production, the magazine won several awards for excellence among a great number of Christian publications of much bigger ministries. Our donors, friends and families regularly send us their thanks and rave reviews.

Such heart, gift of writing, and drive for excellence found their way into his books. After reading this book, by the Spirit's workings, one will most likely fall more in love with missions, native missionaries, and most of all, with the Christ of missions. We thank God for John.

—Bo Barredo, Co-Founder, President Emeritus, and Global Ambassador, Advancing Native Missions

Acknowledgements

Some of the stories in this book first appeared on Advancing Native Mission's website or in *ANM World Missions* magazine that I edited from 2009 through 2018. Though I have edited and updated all these stories and added new ones, I credit the original writers at the end of each story when appropriate. I thank Dee Brookshire for her proofing prowess and ever-present assistance, for William Zodhiates for preparing some of the photos and for designing the cover, for Andrew Needham, Amber Parker and Erica Anderson for overseeing the production procedures, for Krista Darcus or supplying stats, and ANM's regional directors for proofing the stories and making available the original material sent by the mission partners themselves. Above all I thank God for the spiritual and visionary leaders of ANM, Bo Barredo and Oliver Asher, with whom I work.

The cover and Introduction photo is a file photo from Yogyakarta Missionary Training Center. The remaining photos come from the ministries represented. Who actually took the photo is not known.

If any are encouraged to come alongside indigenous ministries, whether ANM's partners or those partnering other agencies who are reaching the unreached in many lands overseas, this book will have served its purpose. Together, may we seek to fulfill Jesus' words, "And this gospel of the kingdom will be preached in the whole world as a testimony to all nations, and then the end will come" (Matthew 24:14).

The Case for Mission

Shouldn't we the native people of alone?
Aren't they happy the way they are?

B efore we start discussing the history of mission or the nature of mission (or missions) or the best way to do mission, we need to have a solid understanding of what mission—or missions—is.

Missions, though technically a plural noun, is often thought of as a singular subject, mission. Mission is a total concept, not a collection of individual incidents. Yet most people think of "missions," a plural noun, but we will consider "mission" or "missions" as a singular subject.

I want to say up front what mission is *not*. It is *not* an attempt to get people of another culture to think like us. It is not a matter of getting them to adopt our ideas and ways or to make them submit to our particular doctrine, though certain basics of belief are expected.

I have heard some people say, "Why bother those people? Leave them alone. They are happy in their own way. Why disturb their culture?"

But are they happy? P. G. Vargis, a native missionary of India, watched a woman throw her baby into the crocodile-infested river. He walked over to her and told her about Jesus. She said, "Why didn't you tell me that 20 minutes sooner?" Millions of people around the world live by centuries-old traditions and superstitions—most of which are oppressive, if not absolutely wicked.

The Hmar tribe in northeast India is an example of what happens to a primitive people when they are introduced to the Bible. They were headhunters and their chiefs decorated the walls of their huts with heads of their enemies. In 1870 the Hmar attacked an English village and walked away with 500 heads, so the British left them alone—and barred anyone from visiting them.

Then one day in 1909 a postal runner brought a copy of *The Gospel of John* in the Lushai language to Hmar chief Kamkhawlun of Senvon village. The chief could not read but eventually found a traveler who could read it to him—though neither of them understood the message. They discovered the name and address of the sender in the back of the book, and invited him, Mr. Watkins Roberts of Wales, to come and explain the book to them.

2

Despite it being against British army orders, Roberts found some young people to take him to Senvon village in Manipur. There Roberts explained the gospel in terms the Hmar could understand. Chawnga Pudaite was one of the first believers. He had a son, Rochunga, who accepted the Lord at age 10. Chawanga charged Ro to get educated and translate the whole Bible for them.

Ro trudged off through the jungle inhabited by tigers, snakes and elephants to the nearest school—96 miles away. When he finished middle school, he went on to college, and then to Allahabad University. He then went to Glasgow, Scotland, to learn Hebrew and Greek and began translating the Bible. He completed his translator training in Wheaton, Illinois, and finally returned to Manipur with a complete Hmar New Testament in 1958. After editing and proofreading, it was published in 1960.

To read the Bible, the Hmar needed to know how to read, so they built nine village schools. Within ten years they opened 85 schools, a college, and a hospital—all without any help from the government. Today the Hmar literacy rate is 85%, compared with 60% for India as a whole.

When their college needed a library, they obtained government funding of 100,000 rupees to build and stock it. But when the governor said they had to stop teaching the Bible in their college, they closed the college rather than forsake the Bible. Still, Hmar graduates became "India's ambassadors, chief secretaries of state, a director general of police, high-ranking officers of the Indian Administrative Services (IAS), doctors, lawyers, engineers, professors and pastors."[1]

---

[1] Cited by Vishal Mangalwadi, *The Book That Made Your World; How the Bible Created the Soul of Western Civilization*, 2001 Thomas Nelson, (cont.)

3

Should Christians have left these worshippers of rivers, mountains, rocks, stars, sun and moon—these headhunters and practitioners of witchcraft and sacrificers of countless chickens, goats and pigs alone? Were these primitive head-hunters suffering from alcoholism, hatred, violence, and poor hygiene, sanitation and nutrition "happy" in their way of life?

Vishal Mangalwadi writes, "Ro believes that only exceptionally callous people would say that his tribe should have been left alone in its (imagined) 'pristine way of life.' The majority would agree that their way of life was sick and needed healing."[2]

We "do missions" not only to bring the good news about Jesus, but to share love, heal the sick, educate their children, and improve their lot in life. In short, sharing that the world is created by a wise and loving God, that the world is good and available for exploration and innovation, and that Jesus, God's Son, died to remit our sins is transformational, as the stories in this book will show.

The first Christians were so excited that Jesus was alive and their sins were forgiven that they couldn't wait to tell everybody about it. So mission, or "missions," first was simply telling neighbors, friends, and city co-dwellers about Jesus. Salvation is found only in him, so we tell people about him. We still go out today to share the "good news" because Jesus instructed his disciples to do so:

Nashville, Tennessee. This and other information on the Hmar is from chapter 19 of that book. The story of Rochunga Pudaite also is wonderfully told in James Heffley's book, *God's Tribesman: the Rochunga Pudaite Story* (Holman, 1977), in Joe Musser, James C. Heffley biography, *Fire on the Hills: the Rochunga Pudaite Story* (Tyndal House Publishers, 19998), additional books, and in the film, "Beyond the Next Mountain."

[2] *Ibid.*, p. 358

Go therefore and make disciples of all nations, baptizing them in the name of the Father and of the Son and of the Holy Spirit, teaching them to observe all that I have commanded you. And behold, I am with you always, to the end of the age." Matthew 28:19-20 [3]

So mission began more as an impelling rather than as a compelling. Mission is primarily carrying, taking, sharing, proclaiming, preaching, or explaining the gospel to people who don't know it, accompanied with commensurate teaching and acts of acts of love and mercy.

That, in short is what mission is and why we do it. The Lord leads on from there, prompting people to start schools, medical clinics, organizations, and much more because we are interested in bringing God's kingdom to earth, as stated in the well-known "Lord's Prayer."

The early disciples and those who immediately followed in their wake were called "apostles" from the Greek word *apostelo*—I send. We get the word "missionaries" from the Latin equivalent—*missio*. Though in modern times the word "missionary" is preferred over "apostle," both have essentially the same function.

Paul said he was called to preach the gospel where it had never before been preached. That is the primary focus of mission today. In today's world, where foreign missionaries are not accepted by many countries, we choose to assist residents of the same or nearby ethnicity and culture to carry out the task. We realize that sending Americans with an advanced (and secularized) western and modern culture could bring a mixed message to those who never heard the gospel. We hope to do all we can to avoid branding Christianity as a "foreign religion."

---

[3] See also Mark 16:15-16, Luke 24:46-48, John 21:28-31.

5

Even though legitimate missionary work is still carried on among people groups that have already received the gospel, the focus today (and ANM's focus) is to reach the remaining unreached, or preach the gospel where Christ is not known. We believe that native missionaries (i.e. missionaries from the "majority" world) are the best qualified to do that in most places.

At the end of 2021, Advancing Native Missions was aiding 13,510 missionaries on the field associated with 292 indigenous ministries that had planted 41,607 churches and were working among 1,466 people groups, most of which were unreached or least reached.

More of the biblical basis for missions is spelled out in the appendices at the rear of this book.

* Some missionaries labor in areas that are too sensitive to mention their names. In such instances, an asterisk is placed after the first mention of their name.

The Man in the Cage

Missionaries came across a man out of his mind, imprisoned in a log jail in a jungle village for five years. What happened next astounded everyone.

Awa* was 35 when he went berserk. He flew into fits of rage and tore things apart. The residents of his Southeast Asia village were terrified.

They consulted the government authorities.

"There's nothing we can do," they demurred.

When Awa's rage continued, the villagers decided there was only one thing they could do. They built a cage out of logs on stilts, somehow got him inside, and then locked the door.

The villagers daily passed food and water through an opening to meet Awa's needs, and cleared the ground under the cage as it became necessary. But Awa still had to live with his torment. This continued for five years.

One day his mother met a team of native evangelists in a neighboring village. They preached about a strange God who they said had all authority in heaven and on earth.

In desperation she approached them and said, "Will you come to my village and help my son?" She told them how he was penned up and why. They agreed to come.

When they got to the village, they gathered the people together and preached the gospel.

"Jesus Christ is the only one who can forgive sin," they proclaimed. "He has power to heal the sick and cast out demons."

After the message, they approached the log cage with Awa inside. They reached through the large cracks between the logs, laid hands on Awa, and prayed for his deliverance.

The villagers invited these holy men to stay the night. So they did, worshiping and praising God past midnight. A few days later they noticed Awa was calm and normal.

"Let him out," the missionaries said.

Cautiously, the villagers let Awa out of his cubicle. Awa was unclothed and stinking.

The villagers let him bathe and gave him some clothes to put on. Throughout the day they witnessed Awa's mind return to wholeness. At the end of the day Awa said to the missionaries, "I want to follow Jesus."

He accepted the Lord, and fifteen members of his family also trusted in Christ.

Like the Gadarene demoniac, he began sharing his story to everyone he met. Soon 35 people of his own village became believers and began gathering as a church.

One day Awa crossed the river and shared his testimony with a nearby village. Another fifteen people committed their lives to Christ. The gospel kept spreading.

Awa's transformation was impressive. But not nearly as impressive as that of the leader who prayed for his deliverance.

Missionary Bono, of another tribe, had been a witch doctor.

"Many evil spirits used to dwell in me," he told an ANM staff member visiting his Southeast Asian country one day. "I could take a red-hot iron bar and lay it across my bare arm and it would not burn me. I could even touch my tongue with it, and nothing would happen."

But one day his own young son became sick with high fever and began convulsing. Bono knew demons had entered his child, so he began going through his incantations and spells, seeking to drive out the demon. But the demon didn't leave; instead, his own child died from the torment, leaving it lying limp in his own arms.

The very next day his mother became deathly sick, vexed by the spirits dwelling in their property. Bono slaughtered seven water buffaloes as sacrifices to the evil spirits. But it was all in vain, as his mother also died.

Bono felt drained of power as he mourned the deaths of his child and his mother. How could he continue as witch doctor, if he, himself, were powerless?

Soon after this a friend from the next village came and began telling him about the most powerful Being in the universe. "Jesus Christ died for your sins, and rose again from the dead," the man said. "And all authority in heaven and earth has been given unto Him. If you commit your life to Him, you, also, will share in His power."

Bono felt he had nothing to lose. He asked Christ to come into his life, and as Christ came in, he felt a strange sensation of many spirit beings leaving his body. "I have a new Resident living inside me," he declared.

After a while, Bono felt he wanted to share the gospel among the people. Having completed only fourth grade, he went to a local leader—now a partner with ANM—who personally tutored him, and enabled the former witch doctor to obtain a Bible degree. That, along with his spiritual giftings, soon made him the leader of 50 native missionaries. They went through the region preaching the gospel to some 100 villages.

It was while preaching the gospel in one of these villages, that the mother of the man in the cage came to him.

That is what missions is all about. Not just obeying a command—though that is important. But setting the captives free, bringing light and love where there is darkness and fear, and transforming people one at a time with the power of the living Christ. That is why we do missions.

Credit goes to Andrew Needham, who wrote the first part of this story for ANM World Missions *in Spring 2017, and to Pete Wong, who supplied "the rest of the story" after personally meeting the leader of the group that prayed for the man in the cage in his Southeast Asian country.*

Heart of an Orphan

Raised as an orphan and imprisoned as a teenage missionary, Angam now joyously plants churches, trains missionaries, and cares for orphans.

"Where's my chicken?" eleven-year-old Angam cried out.

"You're just an orphan," the boy across from him said. "Only those who pay get meat."

The boarding-school children on the other side of the table got served first: rice and chicken with vegetables.

It looked delicious. Then the orphans got theirs—rice and vegetables. Angam was dejected. He had hoped his new home would bring joy. Instead, he felt degraded.

Angam was born into an impoverished home in a small village in Northeast India. His father was a witch doctor and wanted Angam to be a witch doctor, too. But the blood and guts of animal sacrifices disgusted him.

His mother wanted him to go to school, but they had no money. Then when Angam was 9 years old, a missionary came through the village sharing the gospel. Angam accepted the Lord, and the missionary took him to a boarding school where he could learn English. Angam cleaned the rooms and ran errands to pay for his keep.

After three years, the manager said he couldn't pay him anymore, but he could send him to a children's home in a neighboring state. At first that made him happy, but when he got there, he saw that those who could not pay had to sleep in a shed made of bamboo and coconut leaves, while children whose parents paid a fee lived in a nice building with a soft bed.

Angam felt depressed. The meatless meal added insult to his misery. He was so depressed, he even thought of ending his life. He walked over to a nearby cliff, shut his eyes, and stepped over the edge—but some unseen hand seemed to push him back. Again he attempted to step over the edge. This time, in addition to the push back, he heard a voice that said, "You are very important to me." At that point he recommitted his life to God.

I'll be a missionary, he thought.

Starting a missionary journey

From that point on, Angam studied hard, got good grades, and graduated from tenth grade when he was 15. Then he idealistically decided to go as a missionary to Burma. He had no training, but an old man called Uncle Seikho said, "You can come with me."

Angam was happy for the companionship, but the going was tough. Typically, they started walking when the sun came up. They climbed steep hills, ate leaves, and drank from streams along the way.

Around evening they came to Tunklyaw, a village of huts—no restaurant, no hotel.

"Can someone please give us some food?" they asked. "No!"

"Could we please sleep in your house?" "No!"

One householder finally let them sleep on his porch. They were cold, hungry and thirsty. Angam wanted to go home.

"You are a strong man," Uncle Seikho said. "God has chosen you. Never look back."

Then he quoted Galatians 6:9, "Let us not grow weary of doing good; for in due season we will reap, if we do not give up."

So, on they went. For four years they walked from village to village, telling people about Jesus. During the course of that trek, Angam and Uncle Seikho baptized 70 new believers, and gathered three house churches.

Some of the new believers asked questions they could not answer. It made Angam think he should go to Bible college.

"That's a good idea," Uncle Seikho said.

So Angam laid aside his missionary work and began cutting logs for a logging company to earn money for the journey. After a month and a half he had saved the equivalent of $50, and headed to Bible college.

When Angam got there, he had only $13 left, two pairs of pants, and one T-shirt.

After one year, one pair of pants ripped open in back. Angam would wash the other pair and wait for it to dry in the sun before he could go out again.

A month later that pair tore, too. So Angam pretended to be sick. On his bed he prayed, "Dear God, if you are truly my heavenly Father, please get me a pair of pants."

Venturing into ministry

When his classmates came back from chapel, they saw him crying. One of them took his torn pants to a tailor, who stitched them together so he could wear them again. Then the college president returned from a trip to America with a load of used clothes. He gave Angam two pairs of pants and two shirts. He was so happy!

Yet his home state was in unrest. Terrorists attacked his home village, burned the buildings, and killed the pastor and several villagers, including two of his brothers. His parents fled for their lives, but no one knew where. Angam didn't have money to travel, anyway.

After six years, Angam had earned his Bachelor of Theology and Master of Divinity. On graduation day he had to borrow a pair of shoes from a friend to attend the graduation ceremonies. The president surprised him by giving him the "Man of Integrity and Faith" award, along with a cash gift of 1,000 rupees (about $20).

The college also gave him a ticket back to his home state. But it had been in unrest. Terrorists had attacked his home village, burned the buildings, and killed the pastor and several believers. After searching many days he found his family in a different village living like refugees. His father, then 95, had been led to the Lord by Angam's brother three years earlier, just before he was killed. Angam talked with his mother, and she accepted Jesus. Angam used some of his precious cash to buy them some food, and then headed off to Burma to preach the gospel.

Three times he trekked into Burma, and three times he was thrown in jail. The first trip he led a government officer to the Lord. The last time they beat him and put him in a three-foot by seven-foot cell without food, water or blankets with nine other prisoners. They had to take turns sitting down. A lifetime sentence was imposed upon him. The government wouldn't kill him; they would just keep him locked up until he died of exhaustion.

Even so, Angam managed to win one of the prisoners to the Lord. When that prisoner-convert was released from jail, he contacted the first official Angam had led to the Lord. That man came and secured his release. The police took pictures of him and told him never to come back to Burma again.

Returning home, he taught in a Christian school and served as campus minister and academic dean. At the same time, he earned his Master of Systematic Theology and then his Ph.D. in comparative religions. He was well prepared for his life's work.

Beginning an orphanage

One night in 2002, while he was in prayer, the Lord impressed upon him to start his own orphanage and school. His home state was still in turmoil, so he set up headquarters in another part of India, at first taking in a few orphans from his home state.

Once he was trekking through parts of his home area where there were no roads, when they came across a two-year-old child sitting alone in the mud in front of a very small house. Mud covered his legs; his shirt was tattered and full of holes. Mucous dripped from his nose, and tears had made little tracks in the dirt on his face.

Angam learned later that when David was just a tiny one-year-old, militants shot and killed his father while he foraged for food in the nearby forest. David's mother descended into depression; her health spiraled downward, and she soon died.

From then on, David lived with the only family he had left—his elderly grandparents. But they struggled to care for him. His grandfather couldn't climb fruit trees and forage as easily as younger men.

Moreover, a serious ear condition left David with little to no hearing. He couldn't understand anyone who spoke to him, and he didn't know how to communicate with people. They treated him like he was crazy.

Pus leaked from his ears, and the stench was so strong that no one wanted to be near him. Adults and children all avoided him if they could. Little David did not understand why.

Then one day some missionaries native to the land walked past. One of them, Angam, went up to David, and—fighting tears and ignoring the smell—he tenderly wrapped his arms around him.

There was no one to talk to, so they walked away. Near the end of the day, Angam said to his companions, "We need to do something about that child."

It was months later when they returned. This time they were able to talk with the grandparents, who were desperate to find another home for David. So Angam took him with them and placed the boy in the children's home he had started several years earlier.

Papa Angam carefully cleaned David's ears whenever pus would leak out. He took him to the doctor for regular treatment. Soon the infection healed, David's ears stopped leaking, and he began to hear.

His new siblings became playmates and friends. Having experienced the same kind of brokenness from their own backgrounds, they showed him the special love that they had experienced since coming to the home. For the first time in his life, David felt loved.

International Biblical Missionary Church

About this time, he met a young woman named Ruth. She had come from a neighboring state where she was the head of a 300,000-member women's organization. She had obtained a Bachelor of Arts in ministry, a Master of Divinity, and a Doctor of Ministry in coun-selling. Her credentials certainly matched Angam's.

The first time Angam met her, he visited with her for 30 minutes. The second visit he asked her to marry him. The third time they saw each other was when they got married. They now have two biological sons—Jamhaolen, born 2013, and Jamguinlim, born in 2016.

In addition to caring for his own biological family, Angam and Ruth have taken in more than 140 orphans from his home area and reared them in this safe environment. And yes, his orphans get meat!

When they grow up, most of them take training in Angam's International Biblical Missionary Bible School accredited by the Asia Theological Association to bestow B.Th. and M.Div. degrees. Most go on to become missionaries or pastors with Angam's International Biblical Missionary Church.

In 2021, at least 182 missionaries were working with the IBMC. In the previous 16 years these workers planted 342 churches in five countries. They also conduct weekly ministry in 43 mission stations and minister among 180 villages where there is no known believer, no church, and no resident missionary. Many also pastor two or more congregations.

So one orphan, brought to faith by a native missionary, has been used by God to transform the lives of over 140 destitute children, and bring hope and new life to some 27,000 believers. Wherever the gospel has been sown, it has changed lives spiritually and physically, bringing developments in hygiene and education as well. That is why we do missions.

The story of David was contributed by Felisa Needham

He Walked
where Tigers Stalk

His father wanted to sacrifice him to Kali.
Now he serves the King of kings.

D eorao took the child by the hand and led him into the forest. He had the knife. Tonight, he would sacrifice his son to the Hindu goddess Kali. Then, he believed, they would prosper.

Kabir* grew up in a poor village in Maharashtra state of India, the son of peasants. His father, Deorao, struggled to provide for the family through his meager farming. The family worshiped Kali, the Hindu goddess of death and destruction.

Kabir's parents believed if they pleased their goddess, they would avoid poverty and all bad things. So, his family entered into Kali worship unreservedly. The people would gather for religious rituals, beat themselves into a frenzy, and loudly shout their devotion to Kali. Some passed out on the floor.

From his birth in 1962, the first of five siblings, his father and mother took him to these religious gatherings. As Kabir grew, he displayed a natural talent for singing, and his father urged him to join the choral group that sang at religious events. Their songs invited the spirits of the dead to join them. In the worship frenzy, people allegedly heard the spirits speak to them, and they would do anything to win the spirits' favor.

After one of these sessions, Kabir's father felt that if he offered his 9-year-old son as a sacrifice to Kali, everything else in his life would go well. He even discussed this with his wife, Kausil. Surprisingly, or reluctantly, she agreed.

So one night after the religious orgy, Deorao took Kabir to a primitive Hindu temple in the forest. The statue of Kali dominated the small chapel. Deorao carried a knife with which he could perform the sacrifice.

Learning that her husband had taken Kabir to the temple in the woods to perform the sacrifice, Kausil's mother's heart suddenly overpowered her religious devotion. She ran to the temple, grabbed Kabir, and said, "No! Not now!"

The family returned to their drudgery. Life for Kabir was hard. His father beat him, his wife, and the children regularly. Kabir never knew his grandfather. In later life he realized that his father never had a man who modeled fatherhood.

A couple of years later American missionaries Tom and Pat Major visited the village. They worked with a Baptist mission headquartered in a larger town in Maharashtra. The missionary was looking for a yard in which he could conduct a meeting. Many of the villagers refused, but Deorao said, "Sure, why not? More religion will only make one better, right?"

So the missionary set up a meeting in front of Deorao's house. The incident automatically became a village event, and over 100 people showed up. The people, and especially Kabir's family, were impressed by the beautiful Christian songs—sung in Marathi—their own language. And when the missionary spoke, he, also, spoke Marathi. Their hearts were touched.

The missionary came back a second and third time. Deorao was the first person to respond to the missionary's message, and his family followed.

Then trouble began. The villagers didn't like Deorao and his family worshiping another god. Kali would be angry with them and punish the village.

How could the missionary disciple them in these conditions? It was not possible. So the missionary took the family to the mission station miles away. There the mission gave Deorao a maintenance job, and the missionaries conducted Bible lessons for Deorao and Kausil. Though Kabir's father and mother were illiterate, through these Bible studies, they gradually learned to read and understand most of the Bible.

But the relatively tranquil life didn't last long. In 1970 the government started insisting that missionaries of European and British background could not remain as residents. So the missionaries had to leave, and the compound was closed. Where could Deoraj and his family go? Being Christians in a sea of Hindus, and unwelcome in their own village, they fled to the forest and foraged to survive.

They slept under trees on the damp, forest ground. Having only the clothes they wore, they shivered in the cold winters when temperatures dropped as low as 53 degrees Fahrenheit.

"We ate roots of plants, bugs, creeping things," Kabir told me. "Sometimes we gleaned food from farms: onions, berries, plums, guavas."

Bats came out at night and chewed on the fruit. Pieces that fell from their mouths became Kabir's breakfast in the morning. He stole oranges or bananas off farms.

And Deorao was just as mean as before. Without discipleship and without Christian fellowship, his old ways controlled him. "Go work!" he shouted.

Being an "untouchable," Kabir could find only the meanest of work. As a mason's helper, he mixed sand and cement with his bare hands, and then carried the bricks to the mason. The cement dried his skin until it split open, and the bricks made cuts and painful bruises all over his hands; they oozed blood constantly.

The family eventually settled near a garbage dump on the edge of Amravati, where the missionary's organization had been headquartered. One day a man came by, saw the youths scavenging on the dump, and said to Deorao, "May I take your children to an orphanage?"

Deorao and his wife agreed. So the man took Kabir and his two brothers to a Hindu orphanage. But that provided little improvement in their welfare. The Hindus recognized the boys as being untouchables, and treated them accordingly. They got the worst of the food, the barest of accommodations, and sometimes were beaten for no apparent reason.

The man who brought them there occasionally walked past the place. One day Kabir told him how they were being treated. So the man made arrangements for them to be transferred to St. Thomas Orphanage, run by the Church of North India (Anglican). By then Kabir was fifteen. Getting good food, and having decent accommodations was a vast improvement.

But not all was roses. The home sent Kabir to a government school, staffed by personnel affiliated with a right-wing political faction that hates Christians.

"In class, they taught us that the British and white people were murderers," Kabir said. "They never mentioned anything good that they did. Every day they taught us to hate Christians, and soon I began to hate them and everybody!"

Kabir stuck with the school until he finished high school (tenth grade). Then in early 1981, he went to a Christian residential vocational training school, in the state capital.

Though the college was located in the center of Hindu culture, it exhibited strong Christian character and showed respect for each individual. "Brother Kabir, come here," his classmates would call. For the first time, Kabir felt addressed as a real person, not as a thing. He experienced love from his classmates that he never experienced from his father. Kabir's hardened heart began to soften in an environment that respected him as a human being.

In April the churches of the city organized a youth conference. Kabir wanted nothing to do with it, but his friends urged him to attend. "Come sit with us," they said.

Their personal invite warmed his heart, and he went—along with about five-hundred other youths. Well-known gospel singers provided heart-warming songs. Then the speaker stood behind the podium and began to explain that Jesus died for our sins.

I'm not a sinner, Kabir thought. I haven't murdered any-body, or committed any crimes.

Then the speaker began to explain that sin is being angry, saying bad words, taking something that doesn't belong to you, hating people.

These words resonated in Kabir's heart, and when the invitation was given, he went forward, while his friends rejoiced.

The word took effect and immediately began to bear fruit. No one has more zeal than a fresh convert; so Kabir was put in charge of evangelism. He also became a musician in the church, playing the guitar, harmonica, and several Indian instruments.

At the institute, Kabir learned diesel mechanics and air conditioning and refrigeration, and graduated with a Bachelor of Arts in philosophy and public administration, as well.

The call of God was now preeminent in his life, and he next went to Calcutta Bible College where he earned his Bachelor of Theology. After graduating from the college in 1990, he married Sabrina,* and the two of them then went to Northeast India as missionaries.

There Kabir pastored a church, but the environment was not peaceful. The states in Northeast India were torn with unrest and sedition. Once the Indian army raided their house, thinking they might be harboring militants. A short time after that, militants threatened to kidnap his wife and kill his two young daughters.

Kabir and Sabrina decided they didn't need to stay there to be missionaries. They moved to southern India, where Kabir earned his Master of Theology in 1999.

After working a year with the Evangelical Student Union, he returned to Calcutta Bible College in 2000—this time as a teacher. He was loved and respected by the students. The faculty and administration also appreciated him and soon made him registrar and academic dean in 2007.

As if that weren't enough, Kabir also became secretary of Carey Baptist Church, founded by William Carey in 1809. The once-declining church revived with his involvement.

By this time the school was having difficulties. The president left, morale was low, and teachers and students were ready to walk out. The board asked Kabir if he would assume the office of president. He said he would accept the assignment for six months.

Yet even with his teaching and executive responsibilities, he continued to be a missionary at heart. He would rent a boat and go evangelizing on the 52 inhabited islands of the Sundarban Archipelago south of the Ganges Delta.

It's a risky adventure. Tigers live on some of the 100 uninhabited islands, and the big cats don't mind the water. They have been known to sneak up on a fishing boat and grab the fisherman.

Storms struck the region each year. Kabir would take government medical doctors to visit the stricken islanders, bringing drinking water, medicine, food and clothing. Even Muslims welcomed him, young Muslims being especially curious about Jesus Christ.

As Kabir served his now extended term as president of the Bible college, the college regained its footing, and a new president was found to serve long term.

By this time Advancing Native Missions had become aware of his giftings and availability and asked him to become its South Asia Regional Director. Kabir accepted the call and now is the communication link between ANM and sixty-four partner ministries with four thousand missionaries on the field. All these serve among five-hundred people groups. These persistent messengers of the gospel planted six-hundred churches in 2018 and 2019.

So, the boy who was spared being sacrificed to the heathen goddess Kali is now the link between American donors and thousands of missionaries reaching the remaining unreached. A far better outcome.

When the Drug Kingpin
Met the King of Kings

*By Philip Tolman, Co-Director of Seedtime and Harvest
Ministries in Mexico. Chuy, in gray shirt, with his family.*

*Chuy had been a drug addict most of his life. He
sought escape through Christ, but much of his
former life clung to him.*

A t 16 years of age he enlisted in the Mexican army
and was trained as a special agent and secret
service operative. Violence was his life; he lived

to make people afraid of him. After his stint in the army, he drifted off into a deranged world setting.

The progression went from bodyguard services, to mercenary killings and kidnappings, to the drug cartel world. Some twenty years after his stint with the army, Chuy could still open any locked door in under a minute and scale a wall like a monkey. He became a drug king pin in one of Mexico's larger cities, running a shipment line up into distribution channels set up in the U.S. and Canada. He had houses in both the U.S. and Mexico and travelled between them freely through the underground.

This lifestyle had charged its toll. He always travelled heavily armed with AK-15s and semi-automatic machine guns made in Israel, and he knew how to use them. He had been wounded in shoot outs, knifed seven times in the stomach, and he couldn't travel openly anywhere in his territory. Chuy knew that he needed God, but the money, the fame, and the parties were just too attractive.

Over the years he made an acquaintance with Mariano, a local Mexican pastor discipled by our workers. Chuy even donated a piece of land so Mariano could build a church close to his home. He let it be known that the pastor was under his protection, and no one would dare touch him.

Mariano knew that we ran a drug rehab center in another state and brought Chuy to me in the fall of 1993. Chuy wanted to be free from the tyranny of drugs.

Life at the rehab center was not easy. Chuy was not used to letting people tell him what to do, but was very accustomed to telling others what to do. Many times in the next two years we had to stop fights, and Chuy was always in the middle of them. The nightmares and the physical demonic attacks became part of his life as Chuy struggled to break the chains that bound him. Cocaine was the first to go, but other drugs retained their grip on his life. Relapses were common at the beginning. Many nights he found sleep impossible as the fear and the battle waged on. Some substances still wanted to control him until the day he died.

After two years, Chuy thought he was ready to go home. He had never had to save money, as money was always readily available. Now, after two years with no income, what he had was rapidly drying up and he still had a wife and two children to support. Getting set free from drugs was not as simple as he had imagined.

On his own turf his life was still in danger. Drugs were readily available, and he had never done any other type of work. Less than six months later, Chuy was back with his wife and some of his family in tow. "It won't work," he said. "Too many problems back there. I want to live here with you."

Knowing his antisocial tendency and his aggressiveness towards the other people in the center, I didn't think that their living on the mission's compound was a very good idea—but there was no other option. He was back. He had become a new Christian while at the center but his wife and family were not. The next question was, where could he work?

He started selling used and questionable items at the local flea markets and fairs. It was a trickle of income, but it kept food on the table and rent was free. Being among people at the markets, he started to share his newly found faith and freedom. He was very good at that, even though sometimes I thought he was a little forceful.

One day he came to me and said. "I want to study in your Bible school."

I didn't think he would go far with his 8th grade education, but he took our two-year course and learned to preach and use the Word. As his schooling was finishing up, we had a visit from a Mexican brother that had come to know Christ in the USA where he lived. He wanted us to send someone a half-hour drive up the mountains to his home village to preach to his family.

"I'll go," Chuy said. There was no denying him. So we sup-plied him with a vehicle and off he went to start a work. He was firm in his proclamation of Jesus Christ as Savior and Lord, and over the next 10 years believers were gathered, a building con-structed, and the church was established. He was the pastor, and the people loved him.

Of course, Chuy never stopped being himself. When things in our area became dangerous, Chuy appointed himself to be my body guard and followed me around everywhere he could. He never carried a gun again, but just his presence was intimidating. We never had any problems, but much of that was because he let people know that if there were any problems, they would have to deal with him.

Once a pastor from another religious organization came into his town and tried to take some members from his church. One day Chuy met the man on a town street, put his hands around his neck, and lifted him off his feet. He let him know in no uncertain terms that if he bothered his members again things would get worse. The pastor never came back. We know that things are not supposed to be resolved in that way, but Chuy still had his habitual way of dealing with some problems.

The wounds inflicted on him left their stamp. His kidneys eventually stopped functioning, and the last two years of his life he was on dialysis. He continued pastoring until he could no longer make the trip up the mountain to the village. That was one month before he met his Maker. He was 57.

But that's not the end; the story gets better. A year before Chuy went to be with the Lord, his estranged son, who had worked with his dad before running drugs, came with his family to see him. They had not had contact since Chuy left the world of drugs some 12 years earlier. The son stayed with his dad, and he and his family embraced Christ.

Now, 12 years later, they continue to work with us in the ministry. The three daughters along with Chuy's wife are all serving the Lord today and some of his grandchildren are now in ministry. The church that he planted now has a new pastor, and the work continues.

One life was changed, one family transformed, and villagers up the mountain now have eternal life. God must be pleased.

She Taught
the Deaf to Hear

Carmen didn't know that the baby was deaf. Yet she started a reformation that is still growing.

In a dream, Carmen saw a lady come out of a dark cloud and hand her a baby. Carmen began to cry and said, "This is your baby; why are you giving her to me?" Then she heard God's voice say, "Take her; she is your baby. I am giving her to you because I love you."

The dream shocked the newly married woman, who knew she could never have her own baby. Carmen and her husband were with a Gerald Derstine training team in Guatemala. Carmen awoke, crying. *What could this mean?*

Besides the promise of personal satisfaction, the dream foreshadowed a ministry to the deaf that reached around the world. But it would not be without anguish of spirit amid a tremendous move of God.

Carmen grew up in a Roman Catholic family in a small town in Honduras. Her prosperous farmer father wanted to make sure she had a good education. He sent her to grade school in Tegucigalpa, and later to a boarding school run by evangelicals. There Carmen heard the gospel, and longed for a relationship with Jesus, but was turned off by the evangelical's dress and behavior code.

After she graduated from high school, Carmen worked two years as a school teacher in Tegucigalpa and then went to Miami to babysit for a Honduran family. Her father had higher goals for her, and through a connection with a missionary he sent her to a college in Montana.

The last family she stayed with attended a Pentecostal church. As soon as she entered the worship hall, she felt the presence of God. The pastor, named Moses, came up to her, placed his hand on her, and said, "The Lord says, 'I know your prayers, and you have been asking me to show you the true church, but I tell you today, if you come to Jesus, you have found the truth.'"

How did he know? Carmen wondered. She immediately connected with Jesus—without regulations. Suddenly, all she wanted was to do God's will. After graduating with a B.A. in business, she could hardly wait to return to her family in Honduras and share her new-found worldview.

Her parents weren't impressed. They dismissed here as a fanatic—though years later some of them confessed Christ as their personal Savior.

Carmen got a job as a as a bilingual secretary with the Ministry of Education. When she told her boss what kind of church she was seeking, she told her of El Cenaculo Church (The Upper Room). There she excelled in sharing the Four Spiritual Laws with visitors.

A year of miracles

In 1973 Carmen dreamed she was leading a group of young people down the streets of a destroyed town. Dead people lay buried under mud on the streets. People were crying and angry at God for what had happened. Some had lost their whole families. Many refused to hear the word of God, while others eagerly came to Jesus.

The next year Hurricane Fifi hovered over Honduras nearly a week, wreaking great devastation and leaving more than 8,000 dead. The church sent a team to the devastated North Coast. She was living her nightmare. Hundreds turned to Jesus, and more than 5,000 Bibles were handed out, though many failed to respond.

Later that same year the group went to Juticalpa to conduct meetings in a Catholic Church. When they arrived, the priest was gone and the nun in charge would not let the group preach; they could only share personal testimonies and sing.

That night in a dream Carmen saw people sitting on the floor of an upper room filled with people. Some were crying out to God for forgiveness and asking Jesus to come into their hearts. Others were being healed of diseases, while still others were being delivered from demons, and some had an encounter with the Holy Spirit.

The next afternoon they held a small meeting on the second floor of a house belonging to Lydia. Was this the place? They then moved on to the church.

When they entered the church, an elderly blind, crippled woman was sitting on the floor. After several teammates gave their testimonies, the nun left. When Carmen got up to give her testimony, she spontaneously blurted out, "Tonight we will have a Holy Ghost meeting at Lydia's house, and we will pray for the sick."

Immediately the crippled blind lady said, "Pray for me now." They placed her on a chair in the middle of the room and began praying for her. Suddenly she got up out of her chair and began walking and praising God. "I can see!" she shouted. "I'm healed!"

Word spread rapidly and when time came for the evening meeting, the upper room in Lydia's house was packed out. God's presence came down, and people began to cry out to God for forgiveness. Some said they were healed of pain or delivered of demons. One young girl said, "I was deaf, but now I hear!" The whole room was in a holy tumult. By the time the team left, an evangelical church had been planted in Juticalpa.

In 1976 Carmen learned about Gerald Derstine's new Institute of Ministry at Christian Retreat in Bradenton, Florida. Carmen had to return to the U.S. every year to maintain her residency papers, so she went to see what was happening. While there, she heard a voice speak in her head: I will bring you back to this place. I will prepare you and send you all over the world; and you will minister to rich people and poor people. Go back home and tell your people what I am doing here, for I will do the same there.

Carmen loved what was happening at the institute but had no money to enroll. Derstine told her to go home and come back next year. "The Lord will provide," he said. He mentioned the need at one of his evening meetings, and one lady provided the money for her scholarship.

Wedding bells

When Carmen returned the next year, she met a young man named Rodney, also attending the institute. She began to won-der if he was the man appointed for her. Carmen returned to Honduras and got a job at the Honduran Bible Society. There she met Elva Bautista, the Latin America Director for the American Bible Society, housed in the same building. Carmen shared with her how God had been moving in her life and at Christian Retreat. This fed a deep hunger in Elva's spirit, and soon she and her pastor, Roberto Ventura, founded a new church to seek and practice a deeper walk with God. Meanwhile, Rodney visited her in Honduras, and they were married in Tegucigalpa in 1979.

When they returned to Bradenton, Pastor Derstine offered her a job as his assistant secretary. At first she hesitated, because she was hoping to move back to Honduras. "Why don't you try it out for just a year," Derstine suggested. Rodney was already working in the maintenance department, so she decided to give it a try.

The next year, Rev. Derstine gave the staff two weeks off, and Carmen used that time to translate his book, The Kingdom of God Is at Hand, into Spanish. Derstine told her, "Get it printed in Honduras." It was providential.

Several months later, Carmen became secretary to Mac Owen, the Missions Director. Soon after that, when Owen left to go to the mission field, Derstine appointed Carmen to take his position.

Then in 1982 Vlba Bautista visited the ministry to see what God was doing. The church she and Pastor Ventura had founded had grown under God's blessing. Vlba was impressed with the teaching and asked Derstine if he would consider conducting such a ministry in Honduras. Derstine accepted the challenge and asked Carmen to go with him and interpret.

Carmen had never interpreted before, but Derstine said, "Do what God calls you to do; the only thing that can happen is that you just get better at it." So Carmen went with him.

The first institute began in Tegucigalpa in 1983. The moment Carmen got up to interpret, she felt a mantel come over her, and there was no turning back. The school ran for four weeks and about 100 pastors and believers from the region came. The book Carmen translated was distributed to all participants free of charge.

Then calls came in inviting Derstine to conduct similar schools up and down Latin America. Over the next few years Derstine conducted schools in Mexico, Colombia, and Argentina, and places in between, with Carmen interpreting all the way. What the Holy Spirit impressed upon her in Bradenton in 1976 became a reality. She even interpreted for Aida Zacapa, then First Lady of Honduras, when she traveled to Israel to attend the Feast of Tabernacles.

Rodney accompanied Carmen to the school in Guatemala City in November 1983. At the end of the first week, Carmen had that strange dream related at the beginning of this story. Since she couldn't have children naturally, she was thrilled. God had remembered her condition. They immediately went to Tegucigalpa to look for a baby to adopt. But the dream was not to be fulfilled by human efforts. They returned to Bradenton in January 1984.

New arrival

On February 4, the phone rang, and it was Carmen's mother in Honduras. "I have a baby girl for you," she said. "The mother wants to give it to an American couple."

"What?" Carmen could hardly believe her ears. She began dancing around the room and ran to tell Rodney. Then she immediately flew to Honduras to begin the adoption procedure. Being a friend with the Honduran First Lady helped expedite the proceedings. Instead of two years, the adoption took only five months.

Carmen learned the baby was born on December 11. God had promised her the baby before it was born. Rodney met her in Tegucigalpa in June to sign the papers, and together they brought baby Michelle home to Bradenton. What an amazing God we serve!

As weeks went by, Carmen noticed that Michelle was not responding to her voice. Finally, when Michelle was 18 months old, Carmen took her to a specialist and discovered she was deaf. "Lord, why did you give me a deaf child?" Carmen cried out. She fell to her knees and began imploring the Lord, and spent all day praying and crying. At the end of the day, she did not get any particular answer from God—but she had peace in her heart.

Carmen continued to travel through Latin America with short-term mission trips from Christian Retreat, teaching and interpreting, each time leaving Michelle with Rodney's aunt. In one remote village in Honduras, she encountered a deaf child. The girl had no way to communicate with the people around her. She was trapped in silence. Carmen was stunned by the child's communal isolation. God began to speak to her heart.

By then, her daughter, Michelle, was 3. Carmen and Rodney were receiving sign-language classes at home, and Carmen was going to school. Slowly, they were learning how to cope with this crippling handicap.

But the children in Honduras had nothing. No hope, no future—just living in total silence and isolation— treated like non-humans.

Carmen revisited the North Coast and came cross another deaf child while visiting a feeding program for street children. Again, she heard that inward voice, *I want you to start a school for the deaf in Honduras.*

Was that God? She began to cry. She was barely coping with learning sign language for her own child; how could she deal with many deaf children? She tried to ignore the impulse.

As soon as she got home a week later, she sensed a need to get alone with God. She went to her room and closed the door.

I want you to start a school for the deaf in Honduras, the thought came again.

"But God, I'm not a special-ed teacher," she replied. "I don't know how to raise money. I don't like to talk in public." For her, interpreting was fine, but giving her own speeches—no way! Was she sounding like Moses at the burning bush? But God, gentle and kind, told her he would provide. He would give her teachers and everything she needed to start the school. She ended the day relieved. The burden was not hers, but His.

A forgotten people

Starting a school for deaf children in Honduras then became central to her mind and heart. Her first step was to see what already was being done for them there. After some searching, she was shocked to learn that there was:

- no law favoring the disabled;
- no association for the deaf;
- no formal sign language established;
- no interpreters for the deaf;
- only two teachers who knew any sign language at all;
- only one government school that taught deaf children to read lips (no sign language)—but only for ages six to eleven;
- no church for the deaf; and
- no vocational school for the deaf.

The hearing population classified deaf people with the mentally retarded and outcast. Parents of the deaf were ashamed to be seen in public with their children. The road ahead looked bleak—but God was with them.

By faith, Carmen began the school on March 22, 1989. She called together a board of directors in the U.S. and registered it as a non-profit. She later also registered it with the Honduran government. God moved quickly:

- God sent to their doorstep a woman who owned an abandoned house. She allowed them to hold classes there for one year, free of charge.

- Where would she obtain students? She met a pastor who had thirty deaf people searching for vocational training—they became the first students!
- Carmen did not know where to find teachers who knew sign language. God brought the only two teachers in the country who knew any sign language. They became the first teachers!
- She had no idea how to raise the money needed to pay the teachers. God placed a heavy burden on people's hearts, and many prayerful supporters became donors.
- They had no furniture or school supplies. A generous woman from South Carolina donated sewing machines and school supplies and became their first vocational teacher. One of the U.S. board members bought school furniture, and Christian Retreat filled a container and sent it to them.
- People in need became teammates. One doctor came with marriage problems. He found healing and salvation in Jesus Christ, and then volunteered his medical services. He and his wife also counseled young married couples in their church.

After a few years of operating out of small, rented homes, a friend in Honduras donated a big building to them. It was a dream come true. Carmen spent a lot of money fixing it up and customizing it for their special use. But two years later, the friend asked for it back. She took the school to court and won the case, forcing Carmen to forfeit all their improvements. Again they moved into a very small house. Yet God never left them.

In 1989, a lady on a team Carmen took from Bradenton to Honduras took interest in the students and the ministry. After she got home, she sent Carmen a donation of $67. "This is for your building program," she wrote. Carmen had been praying to the Lord to provide finances to build their own school facility, but she had no money designated for a building program. This mustard-seed gift forced the board members to open a building fund account, and they all contributed to it. Things were looking up.

They were also looking down. Rodney and Carmen were having problems with their marriage. He was not interested in learning sign language to communicate with his deaf daughter, and he walked out of the house. They later negotiated a divorce.

Carmen believed all things were ordered by God. At night she lay on the mattress on the floor with Michelle beside her. As a single mother, Carmen continued to raise her daughter, taking her along on her travels—all the while supporting herself. God provided for their needs.

Soon after this, a pastor in Pennsylvania who had been sup-porting her ministry called.

"How you doing?"

"Fine."

"No, really, how are you doing?"

She told him the situation she was in, and he sent her $500. "This is for you, not the ministry," he specified.

Soon after this a friend who lived in Bradenton died. His family, who lived in Maryland, didn't want any of his furniture. So they gave it to Carmen. She then had a house full of furniture, better than before. She became a U.S. citizen in 1991.

By this time Gerald had installed his son, Phil, as president of Christian Retreat. In 1994 the ministry experienced some financial difficulty. That was when

Carmen heard that inward voice, I want you to resign from your job as of July 31. She prayed earnestly about it that night, wrote out her letter of resignation, and turned it in to Phil Derstine the next day.

"Please don't resign," Pastor Phil said. "We will raise the funds to take care of your ministry, and you can continue to administrate it."

"Thank you, Pastor Phil," Carmen replied, "but I have to be obedient to God. God told me to resign, and I have to obey his voice." A week later a friend gave her a check for $10,000 to cover her salary for a year.

Carmen also was gaining a group of followers who provided a continuing measure of support—never an abundant sum, but enough to keep the wheels turning.

Building a dream

The Lord gradually provided funds for the building project. By June 2007 the school had accumulated $100,000 in its building fund. Carmen started looking for property outside Tegucigalpa, which would be cheaper. Amazingly, a property became available inside a gated community in the city for $100,000. It would provide security as well as a place to run a school. She bought the property outright. God's provision!

By 2014, Carmen had another $100,000 in the bank, but still lacked $170,000. The board wanted to have all the funds needed for construction in the bank before groundbreaking, so there would be no stoppage once work began.

In 2014 Beth Meadows from Church of the Messiah in Chesapeake, Virginia brought Abigail Anderson, the Latin America director of Orphans Promise, to visit the school. Abigail viewed the property and looked at the blueprints, and said, "I'm afraid this project is too big for us." Carmen continue to pray and wait on God.

A year later, Abigail called and said they had a sponsor who wanted to provide the $170,000 to complete the funds needed to build the school. Carmen cried and thanked the Lord for his faithfulness! "Faithfull is he who called you who also will do it" (1 Thessalonians 5:24).

So they were ready to build. Years earlier, Engineering Ministry International from Colorado had come and drawn up blueprints for the school—providing a $250,000 service for free. Honduran law now required a Honduran architect had to review and sign the blueprints. A trusted friend referred Carmen to an architect to handle this task. The blueprints were for a two-story building, but there was only enough money for one floor, and possibly a couple rooms on the second. Carmen worked with the architect to accommodate all the elementary and vocational school classrooms, administrative offices, kitchen, cafeteria/multifunction room, and bathrooms on the ground floor. They added just three additional classrooms on the second floor, leaving the building mostly a one-floor structure. There were no dormitories—this was a day school.

The architect had his own construction company and began demolition of the existing structure in November of 2015. A crew from Advancing Native Missions came and helped dispose of the debris. Actual construction started in August 2016.

Everything went well—until the architect started to ask for more money than was stated in the contract. When Carmen asked him to provide receipts for the work done, he refused to do so. He started different areas of the project, but never completed any of them.

Broken ankle, broken promises

Then in January of 2017 Carmen fell in Bradenton and broke her ankle and was unable to travel to Honduras to examine the work. Then the architect stopped construction, leaving the building without a roof, only a few windows installed, and electrical and plumbing begun but not finished.

Carmen hoped God would make everything right again. She hired a lawyer to try to recover some of the funds from the architect, but he refused to pay anything. The lawyer took the case to civil court and after many months of negotiation, the court decided in her favor and ordered the architect to refund $85,000. But the architect still refused to pay, closed his office, and put all his assets in other people's names. Carmen's lawyer has not been able to contact him to this date. The incomplete work also left the building vulnerable to drenching during the rainy season.

After a year of this nonsense, the Lord again performed another miracle. Orphans Promise, which provided more than half of the money for the construction, said that they were able to give another $95,000 to complete the building and endorsed an engineer to head the project. "God never ceases to amaze me!" Carmen said. "His word is true; he has provided for us all along."

In March of 2019, 30 years after founding His Love in Action School for the Deaf, and 12 years after obtaining the land, Carmen dedicated the new building and celebrated the school's 30th anniversary.

But because they built the ground floor with the intention of someday building a second floor, it did not have a proper roof. It needed sealing to keep it from leaking into the classrooms below. A gift for that project was met through ANM as this book was being written; the sealing will carry five years of warranty. Praise God from whom all blessings flow.

God's faithfulness triumphs

His Love in Action is the first Christian school for the deaf in Honduras. It offers both educational and vocational classes to elementary children. Now with nine paid staff and five volunteers, the school provides academic and vocational schooling, Bible training, dental care, uniforms, and hot lunches (Latinos' main meal).

In addition, with God's help,

- The deaf community organized and established the Association for the Deaf, which has since compiled the first Honduran sign-language book.
- While in Congress, Carmen's father helped to pass the first law favoring the disabled.
- The school facility has become a center for counseling, as the Lord draws in passers-by in need of healing comfort or marriage counseling. Many of these seekers have come to know the Lord!
- Schools for the deaf in Honduras multiplied. Many teachers trained at the school now work as principals, interpreters, and teachers in other schools for the deaf in Honduras.
- One graduate returned to his jungle home and started a school for the deaf there.
- An American missionary started another church for the deaf, and former students are now pastors and leaders in that church.

- One went to the North Coast and partnered with an American missionary to start a deaf school in her hometown.
- After American missionary, Noreen Corey, taught at His Love in Action, she went to Equatorial Guinea and opened a deaf school there.
- After hearing Carmen's testimony, a native Philippine pastor, Claudio Cortez, started a school for the deaf in the Philippines.
- During the COVID pandemic in 2021-2022, the school taught sign language via Zoom to many hearing citizens across the country so they could serve the deaf community.
- Most important, the word of God has been preached to the deaf, and now they have the opportunity to become children of the Living God!

In 2021 a donor gave a $100,000 matching gift to complete the second floor, providing rain cover for the ground floor, and provide space for more students and vocational classes. By God's grace, His Love in Action raised the matching funds and construction is ready to begin on schedule in 2022.

God has truly multiplied Carmen's vision to teach these precious children and to share the gospel with them. Those who once were in darkness now see the light! Those who once were chained in silence now have a voice! That's another reason why we do missions.

Lara Sullivan contributed to this article.

They Brave Guns, Drugs, and Warlords

Rosalba and Helman reach a tribe via the Colombia River

To reach Colombia's remote tribes, Helman and Rosalba cross territory controlled by armed guerrillas, drug cartels, and paramilitary forces.

The telephone rang in the ANM office a December morning in 1996.

"They want $10,000," Rosalba Ocampo cried into the phone at the other end. She read from a ransom note she had just received:

"Our commandos are following your steps. You must bring us 10,000 U.S. dollars—alone. If you do not do exactly as we say, your wife, family, home and workplace will be subject to punishment."

ANM responded, "You must leave the country at once. We will help you."

"I don't know where my husband is," Rosalba sobbed, "What can we do?"

"Take whatever money you have and go now. Don't hesitate!"

Rosalba hung up the phone, collected their passports and what few pesos she had, grabbed the children, and called a friend to see if they could hide in his house for the night. Her husband soon joined them and the next day the Ocampo family snuck out the back of the house to a waiting van, where they were covered with mattresses and rushed to the airport. If any of the guerrilla members saw them, they would be dead—or at least held hostage for who knows what fate.

They learned later the guerrilla leaders had held a council of war to determine what to do with this Helman Ocampo who was invading their camps. "If we kill him, he will be a martyr," they said. "Let's kidnap him and hold him for ransom." They took action.

The van arrived at the airport. The Ocampo family boarded a plane, and took off, leaving behind all their personal belongings, which they never recovered. But they had one another.

They landed in South Florida and began living in exile. A church offered them opportunity to minister among the Hispanics in the area, which Helman did for a short while. Yet, after a few months of praying and fasting, he knew he must return.

Historical background

The guerilla movement in Colombia was born in 1960 and soon grew to 10,000 followers. They kidnapped more than 3,000 people, recruited more than 2000 boys and girls, and murdered more than 2000 people. They trained those they kidnapped into armed guerilla fighters. They destroyed many towns, and in 500 municipalities they considered themselves the bosses. A quarter of the country is planted with land mines.

The Revolutionary Armed Forces of Colombia (FARC) tried to make peace with four presidents but made little progress. Then President Santos (2010-2018) gave them virtually all they wanted. President Iván Duque came to power in 2018 and tried to set everything right, but many of the rebels took up arms again and reasserted themselves.

At the same time the fight against illegal drugs didn't fare much better. President Uribe (2002-2010) was able to reduce the cultivation of cocaine from 500,000 acres to 150,000 acres, but it rose again to 700,000 acres again under Santos. President Duque tried to dismantle drug cultivation and its commercialization, but the pandemic halted progress.

Helman and Rosalba Ocampo tread a literal minefield to take the gospel to the unreached tribes of Colombia. They must cross territory controlled by drug cartels and patrolled by bands of militant rebels, while the Colombian army confronts them both. To say the way is treacherous is an understatement. It's amazing they have held on so long and accomplished so much. Their partnership with ANM has been key.

Early childhood

Helman was one of fourteen children born to the rural Ocampo family in Colombia, but five died in their early years.

When he was five, the family sent Helman to live with his aunt in another town because the family couldn't afford to keep him. There he trekked an hour barefoot into town every day to beg for food. Within an hour he would collect all he could carry, and hike back home with his load.

When he was seven, he moved with his family to Puerto Espejo, where he attended school mornings and worked in the coffee fields afternoons. This lasted three months.

"The kids made fun of me," Helman said, "because I wore dirty, patched clothes to school, and had only brown sugar water for lunch. They all had nice clothes and wholesome lunches."

When he was eleven and twelve he worked as a lumberjack and then in the rice fields. He has fungus under his nails today because the water saturated his hands and feet.

Yet his laborious efforts profited him little. He always turned the money over to his dad, who spent 80% of it on liquor, leaving only 20% for the household expenses.

At age eighteen he met a missionary. "I see you are very religious," the missionary said, "but you are missing one thing—Jesus Christ Himself."

As the missionary explained the gospel, Helman fell to his knees and embraced Jesus. For the first time in his life he felt loved.

A call to arms

An American offered to send Helman to the Biblical Seminary, but the seminary required high school completion before ad-mission. Helman had learned to read and write on his own, and had barely been to a real school. They finally worked out an agreement where Helman went to seminary during the day and high school at night.

At age twenty-four Helman got his high school diploma and his seminary degree and began pastoring a church. When he was twenty-six he met and married Rosalba.

"Rosalba was a gift from God," Helman said. "She had the same call that I had to the unreached people groups, particularly the indigenous tribes."

During a period of fasting in January 1981, God spoke to them, saying, "I'm going to save the indigenous peoples through you." Indigenous in Latin America means the Indian tribes, those distinct from people of Spanish background. They formed a ministry called Crisalinco (acronym from the Spanish for "Christ saving the unreached tribes of Colombia"). For the next eight years they traveled together to the tribes and founded a school to train missionaries to reach them.

Often the way was difficult, yet sometimes doors opened wonderfully. One missionary couple set out to reach the Machuna tribe but went without resources. Along the way they met the chief of a Machuna village who agreed to pay their food and transportation costs if they would teach the children how to read. That opened the village to the gospel.

Days of struggle

Then during a church meeting in 1990, Helman felt God calling him to go to the various armed groups in Colombia. This included the drug barons and their henchmen, the armed guerrillas, and the right-wing paramilitary forces. If you crossed any of these groups, you were in big trouble.

But Helman felt clearly that God was calling him and his coworkers to carry Bibles to the armed groups. Within days they were carrying out the commission. Some were kidnapped and held hostage for ransom—and some were brutally murdered. Helman himself was taken several times. "I've buried forty native pastors," he told ANM in 2010. Yet they courageously plodded on.

Things were looking especially bleak for them in 1993. Their locally garnered financial support had decreased. The national churches of Colombia would have been their most logical source of support, but that group was not interested in supporting work among the despised indigenous people.

In order to get some money to live on for themselves and their two daughters, they resorted to sales work in Bogota, desperately striving to earn enough money to support their ministry. They would lay aside what little they could to make trips to the rainforest for two or three months at a time. With few supplies, they traveled down dangerous rivers without life jackets for themselves or their two small daughters. Often, they didn't have proper clothing to protect themselves from the heat and cold. At night they slept in tents that dripped water through the holes when it rained. Then, when exhausted, they returned home.

"We didn't see how we could keep going," Helman said, "but we couldn't give up."

They renewed a prayer they had prayed since the beginning of their ministry: Lord, could you please send someone to come alongside us in the ministry, someone who would partner with us in prayer and finances, and help us accomplish the works you have called us to do?

ANM brought hope

Then in 1994 Helman and Rosalba received a telephone call from Advancing Native Missions. Someone had told ANM about their ministry, and the leaders wanted to visit and learn more about them. Hope spoke in a whisper, Was this the answer to their prayer? The Ocampos invited them to visit.

Later that year ANM's Graham Stewart and Danny McAllister visited the Ocampos. "What impressed me," Danny recalls, "was the Ocampos' willingness to sacrifice everything—even their lives—to advance the gospel."

Danny and Graham expressed ANM's sincere passion for helping native missionaries spread the gospel and minister effectively in their homelands. A new and lasting relationship was quickly formed. Small but regular financial support from American donors began to flow in through ANM, and Helman and Rosalba expanded their network of training centers and church planters.

It was just in time. Barely two years later they received that ransom note and ANM provided their emergency evacuation tickets. Of course, Helman subsequently returned to keep the work going.

Helman and the missionaries still work in danger. In 2010 a mission team heading down river to witness was ambushed by terrorists, who demanded their gasoline. When the team re-fused, the terrorists grabbed and bound Pastor Emilio, put him in a canoe, and headed up river. Then the terrorists returned and threatened to kill them all for spreading the gospel. The team stood their ground. Mysteriously, the terrorists left, and the team continued their journey. Two days later they found Pastor Emilio's body in the bush with multiple blows to his head.

In early March of 2020 student-missionary Carlos went to the jungle area to meet with the Nukak indigenous people to learn their language. Then the COVID-19 pandemic hit, and all open transit was closed. What began as a two-week visit turned into a two-month residency. He began to learn their language and learned to fish and hunt the way the Nukaks did. They began to trust him so much they invited him to their decision-making meetings. Some began attending Bible studies and were fascinated with what he shared. After two months, Carlos had to return to Bible school to continue his training. Besides Carlos, Loyda, Barbara, and Christian are now learning the Nukak language. Crisalinco workers have been working in this area for six years and believe the nomadic tribe of hunters and gatherers are on the verge of receiving the gospel.

The Nukaks have no way of earning money. Though some worked for the cartels, they were paid with cocaine. So still having no way to buy food or goods, they then became addicted. Since some resort to stealing, people in towns at the edge of the jungle want them expelled from their area. There is no sympathy for these Nukaks. Only the Ocampos and their selfless missionaries care for their souls. Persevering through many hazards and obstacles, the missionaries press on, and have accomplished much with ANM's partnership.

There are sixty-three tribes in Colombia, each with their own language and culture. Some of the larger tribes, such as the Sikuani, have up to 2,400 communities. Crisalinco has trained 350 indigenous pastors, leaders and missionaries among the Sikuani, located in southwest Vichada, and each of them has planted one or more churches.

Crisalinco has established seven on-the-field missionary training centers for training indigenous workers. So far it has trained 350 missionaries, indigenous pastors and leaders who have planted 500 churches among fifty tribes or people groups. Brandon Hill, married to Helman and Rosalba's daughter, Deysi, estimates that 90% of Colombia's tribes have experienced a meaningful introduction to the gospel from Crisalinco and other ministries working among the indigenous. Only 10% are truly unreached.

"We have translated 'The Life of Jesus' into twenty-seven languages and continue to train [indigenous workers] so the Indians can continue to translate the Bible into their own dialect," he said.

In addition, Crisalinco founded and ran for a time a refugee center keeping approximately a hundred children safe from guerrilla kidnappings and providing comfort and aid to widows and their children. They later turned it over to another ministry.

Helman lost his brother-in-law and mother to the COVID-19 pandemic of 2020. At the same time, the tribal leaders he had trained reached out among their own people and the work kept moving forward. Helman and Rosalba sense the support and prayers of God's people in

America. "Like many others in this world, we pay a high price for following Jesus, but you and your prayers make a big difference," Helman said.

The hardships, trials, dangers, and challenges of Colombia have not ended. Yet Helman, Rosalba, and the workers of Crisalinco continue wholeheartedly to pursue their call to spread the gospel among, minister to, and aid the unreached tribal groups of Colombia. Along the way, drug lords, rebels, and the Colombian military also may get a dose of the gospel. That's the way missions work.

This chapter is based on articles written for ANM
Magazine *by Lucille Lebeau in 2010 and
by Matthew Shareff in 2016.*

Transforming Togo
—One Child at Time

He was saved at 12, baptized when 14, and felt the call of God on his life at 18. He now operates a school for 1,000 children. But he had a bad start.

O ne-year-old Kodjo Bossou shrieked in pain as the nurse injected the needle into the young boy's hip. Suddenly everything went quiet and the nurse's face turned ashen. "I've severed a nerve," he murmured. "He'll never walk again."

The voodoo followers of his village believed Kodjo had been cursed. Yet instead of becoming bitter from the shunning and teasing, Kodjo felt compassion for others who suffered. Through determination and hard work, he began walking two years later. But his left leg always remained smaller and shorter than the right leg. He still walks with a severe limp.

In 1973, his father, who was principal of the local government-run school, developed a headache and came home early. The next day he died without any explanation. Unable to provide for her three children in their rural village, Elizabeth, Kodjo's mother, moved to Lomé, the capital of Togo, a city today of 800,000, to live with her father. The whole family jammed into his one-bedroom house: Elizabeth, three-year-old Kodjo, his five-year-old brother, Innocent, and three-month-old Christine.

The grandfather worked for a road construction company, but his hard labors could not provide for the whole family. Elizabeth did everything she could, but they struggled. The closest middle school was a privately run school nearly five miles away, and there was no bus service. Kodjo walked to school in the morning, walked home at noon for lunch, then went back again at two, and came home at five. Kodjo could go to school as long as he could pay the fees. He also had to buy his own textbooks and readers.

Kodjo remembers, "Life was miserable for us. At times there was no food or shelter. I wore the same shirt for three years. Momma would sell things and I could go to school for a time, but then money would run short and I would be kicked out. The last thing she sold to further my education was her wedding ring. The sadness of being sent home from school because of poverty never left me."

At age nine, Kodjo got a big gas can, filled it up with kerosene, and carried it on his head door-to-door selling it by the liter. If he ran out of money, the school expelled him. That's why he didn't graduate from high school until he was twenty-five. Innocent quit school after the ninth grade, and Christine went only as far as fifth grade.

The school crowded as many as 120 students into a single class. Kodjo had sixty-five students in his ninth-grade class. Yet Kodjo was the top student in that class and scored the highest in the nation in the national exam. He was an intelligent and hard-working student; only poverty hindered him. Despite his economic and physical handicap, he was determined to do well.

Kodjo was growing spiritually as well. He and his siblings attended Vacation Bible School conducted by Pastor Fields, an American Baptist missionary. When Kodjo was twelve, Pastor Fields led his brother, Innocent, to the Lord, and Innocent then led Kodjo to Christ. Kodjo was baptized when he was fourteen, and at the age of eighteen he felt God calling him to serve him in ministry.

Yet his personal desire was to be a doctor. So, after he graduated from high school, he immediately enrolled in the University of Lomé, commuting by half-hour bicycle ride each way. He supported himself by doing laundry: handwashing the clothes, drying them on a line, ironing them, and returning them to his clients.

But he didn't have peace. Finally, after two years of college, he surrendered to the will of God and enrolled in Mount Horeb Bible College to prepare himself for ministry, all the while supporting himself as a laundryman.

After earning his Bible college degree, Kodjo taught Sunday school, preached, recorded a gospel radio and TV program, served as an assistant pastor, and worked as a missionary with Child Evangelism Ministries based in Indiana for eight years. According to Kodjo, believers were strengthened in their walk with the Lord, and unbelievers became Christians. He was popular with society and often was asked to emcee weddings and dedications. Many churches asked him to help with Vacation Bible Schools and puppet shows. He met Abla in church, and they married in 1998. God blessed them with three sons.

Move to America

Kodjo longed to change the impoverished situation of his family, so he applied to come to the U.S. for work. In 2009, a host family in Ottumwa, Iowa, offered to take all five of them in, and a meatpacking plant there offered him and his wife jobs. He promised his Togo family and friends he would one day return to help them.

Still having a desire to get some kind of medical training, Kodjo went to nursing school outside work hours. Upon obtaining his LPN, he applied to a Christian rehabilitation and skilled nursing facility run by Good Samaritan Society. This new job gave him the opportunity to do what he loved most: care for people. The residents loved him. He talked, hugged, and prayed with them.

And he still cared for the people of Togo, especially the children. He and his wife, who also had gotten a better job, decided to live on her salary and use his paycheck to begin a ministry in Togo called African Kids Evangelism Ministries.

The first thing they did was to buy some land in Togo. In 2015, Kodjo returned to Togo with some friends from

Ottumwa intending to build a wall around the property —necessary in Africa to keep out stray animals.

After installing the fence, his friends said, "Let's build some classrooms and get this school going." They called their credit card company in America to advance them the funds, and they built three classrooms. His American friends also hand-built the first forty-six desks. The school opened that year with ninety-nine students in pre-K through second grade. Kodjo did not want any little boy or girl to be sent home from school because they could not pay, so he charged them nothing. The seed of Christ was being planted in their young lives.

Some of his helpers in Iowa also were Advancing Native Missions supporters. They thought Kodjo would be a good match for ANM and brought him to visit the office in Virginia. The staff and leadership there discovered the heart of this humble, selfless man and came alongside him. Others in the ANM community heard of his dreams and came on board to help add their support to Kodjo's sacrificial gift to the needy in his country.

Today, a three-story building provides facilities to educate twelve-hundred students in classes pre-K through the ninth grade in Djagble, a community of about thirty thousand.

"My goal is to go through twelfth grade," Kodjo told me, "but high school teachers cost more."

Now he had the attention of the whole community. His Iowa friends helped him obtain a color TV and a DVD player, and he began showing Christian movies on Wednesday and Saturday nights. In each viewing, he would pause for 20 or 30 minutes and explain the gospel. People started yielding their lives to Christ, and the new believers started meeting for church in one of the classrooms. Today, a congregation of 300 enthusiastic believers worships at the church in Djagble.

Journey to the countryside

One afternoon Kodjo decided to take a van and show his American friends how people lived in the rural villages. Kodjo started driving, not having any particular destination in mind. During the two-hour ride they noticed mosques alongside the road almost every five to ten minutes. After an hour-and-a-half of driving, Kodjo parked the car and said, "O.K., let's go." They all got out of the car and started walking along a narrow path.

One of his friends asked, "Where are we going?"

"I don't know," Kodjo replied. "I've never been here before."

Then they met a woman. Shocked to meet a group of white people in the middle of the jungle, she said, "Wait here. I want to call my husband."

She returned with her husband carrying a large machete in his right hand. Kodjo introduced himself in the local language, and the man relaxed and smiled and put away his machete. Kodjo asked him his name, and he answered, "Kodjo." Every-one looked at each other, astounded. Kodjo smiled and said, "That's my name, too." That's what they call a boy born on Monday.

The village was called Nyamtougoukope and was about the same size as Tsave. He showed the group his family, his house, their rooms, the kitchen, and his farm. After the friendly visit, as Kodjo and his friends were getting ready to leave, Kodjo the villager said, "Please don't forget us."

"I'll be back," Kodjo said.

The next year, the same group returned, bringing clothes and medicine. This time they saw something shockingly different: Someone had built a mosque in the village. The local Kodjo came from his farm, welcomed them, and introduced them to his brother, Baco, who was chief of the village and a Muslim.

Kodjo asked Chief Baco if he could call the village together to tell them something. The chief gathered the villagers, and Kodjo preached the gospel. More than a hundred people accepted the Lord. Kodjo and his American friends gave out the clothes and medicines, and the villagers rejoiced.

The chief was so happy that he later donated 2.4 acres for a church so they could construct a church meeting hall. Kodjo's friends from Ottumwa chipped in with funds to construct a church building and drill a well for the community. Though the chief continues to maintain his Muslim identity, he now worships with the congregation.

Kodjo returned to America and shared the developments. A church provided forty-one goats for members of the new church and a fifteen-passenger van to facilitate evangelistic and discipling ventures. American volunteers went and conducted two health clinics there.

The church at Djagble sent a team to encourage the believers and appointed Daniel, from Djagble, as pastor. Today the village of Nyamtougoukope has a congregation of 150 believers meeting in a church structure standing next to a mosque that now stands empty.

Daniel originally was from the village of Tsave, a village of about 3,000 some hours north of Lomé by car. He decided to go talk with Ake Agosse, the local chief there. As he entered the village, he noticed the voodoo idols everywhere. "I do my best to settle disputes among the villagers," Chief Agosse said, "but Islam and their voodoo traditions do not bring me peace."

While Voodoo has a strong hold on the people of Togo, Islam has found its way into nearly every tribe and community in the nation. Neither worldview offers true peace and joy and the mix often brings confusion.

Noting the chief's comments as a signal, Daniel began telling the chief about Jesus Christ, the Prince of Peace. By the end of the day, Chief Agosse and six of his village elders had trusted Christ as their Lord and Savior. They gladly gave Daniel permission to return to present the gospel to the whole village.

Four weeks later, Daniel filled his newly acquired fifteen-passenger van and brought members from the Djagble church to share the gospel. They showed the "Jesus" film in the local Ewe language and saw 108 villagers place their trust in Jesus Christ. A new congregation, including Chief Agosse, now worships the Lord Jesus Christ in Tsave village.

When another piece of land beside the school went up for sale, Kodjo purchased it with funds provided by a Charlottesville Church. The actual construction of the clinic awaits funding. He also started putting together a chicken farm to produce local income for his ministries; it, likewise, awaits further funding before it can become operational.

Sometimes the Lord gives us surprise challenges. When Kodjo visited his ministry grounds in August 2020, he learned that the government was requiring him to pay $22,000 of back-pay pension deposits for his teachers. He made an emergency call to his friend in Iowa, who was able to send him a $2,000 advance to satisfy the government officials and allow the school open. Yet even if that challenge is fully met, there will surely be others.

Astounding development

Even so, the rapid development is astounding. ANM's regional director for Africa, Lou Mancari, blurted, "All this has happened in just the past five years! Most ministries take ten to fifteen years to get to this point. This is such a God thing."

And much of that development is the fruit of Kodjo's part-ners in Iowa and Virginia.

Kodjo's employer, Good Samaritan Society, supports his ministry by allowing him two to three months' leave every year to return to Togo to keep his ministry growing. The director said, "You can see Christ working through Kodjo and through his spirit. You can feel it—in his smile, in his eyes, in the way he talks about the staff, residents, and his mission."

Kodjo brought his Momma to Iowa ten years ago to care for the boys when they were younger. David, now twenty-two, is assistant coach of the Ottumwa High School while continuing his education and Jonathan is enrolled in Central College in Iowa. Kodjo's mother went back to her native Africa in 2020 and is happy to be back in her natural environment. Kodjo and Abla make sure one of them or David is home when Joseph, now eleven, is home from school.

When you ask Kodjo, who turned fifty in 2020, what he thinks about all that God has done, his only reply is, "My prayer is that God uses me as a good example."

It seems God is answering his prayer. Kodjo hopes someday to return to Togo to work full time with the ministry.

When Kodjo was a child, medical care and education were the hardest things to get, and the saving grace of Jesus was rarely heard. Kodjo wants all this to change for as many people as possible. So does ANM. Again, that's why we do missions.

Much of this article was first written by Dee Brookshire and posted on the ANM website, updated by John Lindner.

They Show the Way
in Indonesia

Paulus embraces the imam who defended him against false charges by radical Muslims.

A former mischievous Muslim boy and a gracious ex-Muslim girl now bring life to many in the world's most populous Muslim nation.

A mob furiously made its way with sticks and torches towards the unfinished church building. Sri lived in the house next door with her pastor-husband, Paulus. "Allah Akbar! [God is greater!] Burn it down! Burn it down!" they shouted.

The year was 1995. The village, Maguwo, on Java Island. The country, Indonesia. Muslims across the nation were mounting an anti-Christian jihad.

Sri heard the commotion growing louder as some 20 to 30 people drew near. The acrid smell of the kerosene torches filled the air.

It was 10 o'clock at night and Paulus was in West Java on business. All four of her children were already in bed, sound asleep. When the noise seemed to subside slightly, Sri opened the door.

"Allah Akbar!" the demonstrators shouted, intent on breaking into the building under construction and burning it to the ground.

Sri knew the Maguwo residents and they respected her. These torch-carrying radicals were from another village. The torches cast threatening flickers on the enclosed but still unfinished church structure and lit Sri's face as she walked toward the building.

"You want to destroy this church building?" she confronted them in a loud voice. "Then you will have to do that over my dead body!"

The crowd was stunned. They had planned arson, not murder. The beautiful young woman stood her ground between the demonstrators and the building. Slowly, one-by-one, they put down their torches and left.

Her neighbors told her later they were watching from their windows, ready to rescue her if the need arose. Her gentle spirit and her thoughtful, teaching ways had endeared her to the women of the village.

When Paulus returned, she hugged him. "It was a good thing you were away," she told him calmly. "If you had been here, no telling what might have happened!"

Paulus was born Trimanto Wibowo, on August 4, 1948, in Winong Kota village, founded by his grandfather. The third child of a devout Muslim family, he was an incorrigible mischief-maker. He would visit the mosque during prayer time and swat the men on their behinds while they were bowed over in prayer. The enraged imam banned him from the mosque.

Child mischief-maker

His parents thought he was possessed and as a last-ditch effort took him to the witch doctor. In desperation his father forced him to utter the oath: "If I do not stop and repent of my misdeeds, I will be a cripple all my life. Allah Akbar!" And then banished him from the village.

But something else was happening. Even before Trimanto was expelled from the village, his older sister came to faith in Christ and was baptized in the Mennonite church three miles down the road. She dragged Trimanto to Sunday school, but after six months he quit going.

She gave him several tracts, including "The Way of Salvation" in Javanese. He thought it interesting and stuck it in his pocket for later reference. Meanwhile he sabotaged her bicycle and threw stones on the metal church roof when she attended prayer meetings. He borrowed books from the church and never returned them. He even spread malicious rumors denigrating the Christians. Yet the Mennonites never retaliated; they just loved him. It made him wonder.

73

Then came the banishment and the next two years he worked as a water-buffalo boy. He fell off the buffalo at least a dozen times and was hit several times by the buffalo's horns. Finally, after two-and-a-half years he returned home to begin high school.

That was when the Holy Spirit gently broke through his mischievous spirit. The kindness and patience of the Mennonite believers wooed his heart. One night, at the age of 14, Trimanto pulled out that tract he had been carrying around so long. At the end were four steps to follow to accept Christ as his Savior. Trimanto prayed the prescribed prayer and knew that Jesus had come into his life. He began reading other tracts and studying the Bible fervently and five years later he told an elder in the local church he wanted to be baptized.

His mother was the daughter of the principal of the village boarding school, who had taken the hajj to Mecca. She told him if he forsook Allah, he would never know prosperity. Others dismissed his request. "He just wants to see the pretty girls in the church," they said. Ultimately, his father, a Javanese Muslim mystic leader, told him, "If you want to be a Christian, never play a game at it."

Trimanto persisted, and the Christian ladies at church were delighted. At his baptism they named him Paulus, because they considered his turn-about similar to that of the apostle Paul's. People, especially his mother, were surprised when they saw his changed life. He truly became a "new creature" in Christ.

After finishing high school, Paulus studied history at a Christian university, but left early to attend Spreading Gospel Bible School in Majalengka, West Java in 1970. A year later he began working as an itinerant evangelist and church planter. He conducted open-air meetings with village churches and followed them up with Bible studies and house prayer meetings.

One day in 1973 he was taking an Australian couple to visit some ministries in a rural area. When he came to Jelok he saw this beautiful young lady teaching children how to sing, "Jesus Loves Me." He had no idea she was a Muslim.

The beautiful young lady

Sri similarly was born into a devoted Muslim family in Boyolali, Central Java, the sixth in a family of 11 siblings. She grew up a good Muslim going to the mosque every day, observing all the Muslim rituals, and teaching the Quran to the children.

Sri suffered from near-constant attacks of vertigo. One day when she was 19, a concerned neighbor, an elder of a nearby church, approached her one day and asked, "Why don't you come to our church?" So she went to the church in Jelok, about two-and-a-half miles down the road; the pastor prayed for her, and she was healed.

Sri was happy with her healing but drew no other conclusions. She did not think about who God was, much less who was the God that her neighbor's pastor had prayed to. Yet she felt comfortable frequenting the place where she was healed.

One day, the pastor offered, "I'll provide a scholarship for you to become a teacher in our religious education program." While Sri still did not know who the pastor's God was, she said, "All right. I'll take it."

After finishing the one-year course, Sri came back and taught in the church's religious education program for two years. "In my heart I didn't know who Christ was," she admitted later. "I didn't know who the Savior was. I didn't know at that time what it meant to be a Christian. I just taught Christianity like any other subject."

During this time, she lived with her sister in Jelok, prayed the Muslim prayers five times a day, yet went to church on Sunday and read the Bible in her room every night.

It was at that point that Paulus visited Jelok and noticed the beautiful young lady teaching the children that song. Neither anticipated it, but God would bring them together again in the not-too-distant future.

By this time, Sri's family had become disturbed over the pastor's attention toward their daughter. Neither did they like her frequenting the church. They decided to clamp down on her, even though she still had no idea what being a Christian meant. Whenever she went home to Boyolali, her family refused to let her step inside the house; she had to spend the night outside on the porch.

At the same time, the pastor was keenly aware that the family would try to secure Sri's loyalty to Islam. In order to preempt this, he advised she get more training at the Bible school in Majalengka, and she consented. When her family learned about that, they told her, "Stay there, and don't ever come home."

After her first three months in Bible school she faced the truth that there was no salvation outside of Christ. Deeply struck by this revelation, she yielded her life to Christ.

In Sri's ninth month in the school, two missionaries, one American and the other Indonesian, came to visit. The American missionary taught while the Indonesian missionary translated. The Indonesian missionary was Paulus Wibowo.

Someone told Paulus, "There is a new student on campus. Why don't you meet her?" The next day, when the students came for prayer at 4 a.m., Paulus stood in front of the chapel.

When she appeared, it was the same lovely lady he had seen in Jelok. He boldly asked, "Would you like to serve the Lord with me in the future?"

Caught completely off guard, Sri simply replied, "His will be done," and rushed into the chapel.

The next day he sent her the best gift a poor missionary could afford: a bar of fragrant soap.

At this point, Sri was hardly interested in developing any relationship with the visiting Indonesian missionary. She thought he was brash to speak so openly.

Then she began to think, If I do not agree to his proposition, I may not have any other chance to marry a Christian man. Soon I may have to go back home, and my family will likely force me to marry a Muslim.

Paulus knew that Bible students sometimes could not afford the simple things. So for the next five months he sent her presents of detergent and shampoo. Eventually, Sri relented, and they were married in Boyolali on January 7, 1975. God had joined them together for a purpose.

In visiting many rural church plants by Indonesian workers, Paulus was convinced he should obtain an M.A. in missions and an M.Div. for pastoral ministry so he could better advise local workers. At the same time he pastored a local church.

Expanding the vision

He and Sri and their four children moved to Bandung in March 1982 and became pastor of a church and shared the gospel from village to village as well as among the Chinese in town. At the same time, he earned his M.A. and M.Div. at Tyranus Bible Institute there. After graduating in 1982, he took a teaching position in Christian University and Theological Seminary in Yogyakarta and helped coordinate the church planting of students. During the next few years, Paulus attended several international missions conferences, including Billy Graham's International Congress for Itinerant Evangelists in Amsterdam in 1983.

Then he attended the Lausanne II meeting in Manila in 1989 and met Bo Barredo and Carl Gordon, who subsequently cofounded Advancing Native Missions. Their conversation rekindled the evangelistic flame in Paulus's heart that had nearly gone out.

He returned from Manila energized to see the gospel reach every nook and cranny of Indonesia. He began scouring the countryside to see which areas were open to the gospel and which were not.

"I visited church planters, saw their impoverished living conditions, and realized how much good could be done with a little amount of support," he said. "I longed to help them."

What Paulus saw transformed his life and prompted him to do two things: In 1993 he resigned his position at the university to become the Indonesia liaison for Advancing Native Missions. That same year he began Yogyakarta Missionary Training Center to provide the practical kind of training he realized those entering the ministry needed.

Besides teaching the basic doctrines of theology, Christ and salvation, the school also taught practical subjects like how to make an initial visit to a community, how to make their first contact, how they could assess their own assets in order to plan how they could sustain themselves until a congregation was formed. After a period of intensive training, they were sent out to practice what they had learned. After a year, they would return to get their questions answered and complete their training. Only after this were they sent out as itinerant evangelists and church planters all over Indonesia.

Meanwhile his wife, Sri, began a ministry for new believers in Maguwo village. She began with five Muslim women. Her gentle spirit and Christian education training enabled her to share the truth about Jesus Christ in a winsome way. The group grew until there were 55 baptized believers. They formed the nucleus of the Maguwo village church.

At the same time Sri's upright life and gentle ways endeared her to the people of the community, who elected her community treasurer. "I'll take the job only if anyone who borrows money from the community is required to pay it back," she said. All agreed.

Within one year all persons who had borrowed money from the community funds paid it all back.

Reversal of attitude

As Sri continued meeting with various groups of people, mostly women, her discreet conversations, gentle attitude, gracious style of living, and willingness to be an agent of change helped open the eyes of many to what Christianity really is.

Then, early in 1995, during a nation-wide rise in anti-Christian sentiment, some of those hostile to Christianity began to spread false rumors about them, and their neighbors even refused to speak with them. They prayed earnestly, "Lord, if we did anything wrong, please show us what it is."

Soon after that a village chief and his wife paid them a visit. "We trust that the accusations are false," they told them, and then he shared an Indonesian proverb, "Gold is still gold, even if people throw mud on it."

Tensions between Christians and Muslims eventually boiled over and Muslims began attacking Christians and burning and looting of churches. That was when the crowd came to burn down Paulus's nearly completed church building.

After this frightening episode, the warm feeling among Christians and Muslims in the community returned. Just before Christmas 2009 their neighbors came to them and said, "Why don't you put a sign in front of your church? That way people will know where to go for worship on Sunday."

So Sri and Paulus erected a sign atop the front door. It said, "Meeting place for worship of Christ Congregational Church of Indonesia," Maguwoharjo, Yogyakarta. All things come together in God's time (Ecclesiastes 3:11).

Even though local conditions smoothed, planting churches was not as easy as before. Open-air meetings like Paulus held in the 1970s and showing the "Jesus" film as he did in the 1980s was now taboo. Now they could publicly speak of Christ only at funerals and weddings.

And constructing a church building required the signatures of seventy-five neighbors. Getting that many signatures from a dominantly Muslim community was nearly impossible—unless the Lord led the way.

One man had been praying and fasting for a certain village. One day he met a man from the village and shared Christ with him. The Lord opened his heart and he trusted in Christ. He went home and led his whole family to the Lord: Nine new believers!

The group soon grew to thirty, and they are praying that theirs neighbors and friends will also embrace Christ.

Christians in another village suffered great persecution. Three times they built a church building, and three times Muslims came and tore it down. What could the believers do?

They decided to hold their meetings in the house of a believer in the center of the village. When a drought hit the area, all the wells in the village dried up—except the well of the believer in whose house they were meeting. The Christians invited their Muslim neighbors to help themselves to the water from the believer's well.

Now their former enemies are suggesting the Christians build a church building inside the village, and they even offered to help dig the foundation. No less than 125 Muslim neighbors signed the request, allowing them to obtain the legal permit to build.

"Without Him we can do nothing, but with Him all things are possible," Paulus said.

Many times trials, persecutions, disappointments, and misunderstandings by fellow servants of the Lord tempted him to give up. Their eldest daughter, Wiwid, left the family tradition and married a Muslim. But she maintained her Christian testimony and walk with the Lord. Some years later, her husband, Wawan, confessed faith in Christ. Wiwid obtained a Ph.D. in geography from Australia and today is a professor of geography in a university in Yogyakarta. Wawan supports the work as a businessman.

Daughter Tutik is an administrator and her husband, Hayu, is an instructor in a mine company. The youngest son, Yonathan, observed his doctorate in information technology in Bangkok.

Where do we go from here?

Some may wonder what will happen to the ministry when Paulus and Sri are no longer able to provide leadership. God has thought of that, too.

Their older son, Daniel, is rising to leadership. But it wasn't always that promising.

Growing up in a Muslim-dominated community, Daniel became bitter over his Christian orientation. As the only Christian in the local school, he was maligned by his Muslim peers, who wouldn't even play with him on the playground. He walked a half-mile out of the way going home so he wouldn't have to take the jeers of Muslim young men along the main road. He felt no comfort in his Christian heritage, even though friends and visitors often told him, "You are a kind and thoughtful young man. You'll be a beloved leader."

He just shrugged and said, "I prefer to work in the background."

Daniel admitted later he was a hardened, bitter young man. "I hated church. I hated people. I hated those radical elements. I hated life."

And then one day an accident provoked a change in his outlook. He and his friend hopped on their motorbikes to get to class. When the friend passed him, Daniel goosed his bike to regain the lead, but took the next corner too fast and he and his bike slammed into a wall.

Daniel was knocked unconscious. When he regained consciousness and tried to get up, severe pain struck his abdomen. He looked down and his abdomen had turned dark purple. Blood oozed from his mouth and a piece of helmet stuck to his face. His friend flagged down a passing car, and the driver took him to the nearby military health center.

The military center did not have facilities to treat his severe wounds, so they transferred him to a larger hospital. All the ER rooms were occupied, so they put Daniel on a gurney and wheeled him into a storage room. It had no air conditioning, and Daniel sweltered in the 91°F heat. He wanted a drink but couldn't swallow. Nurses inserted a tube up his nose and another in his mouth. He lay in agony for six hours.

Finally, an air-conditioned room became available. Somewhat refreshed by the coolness, he reflected on his past and where God was taking him. Some thought his accident would harden his heart against God, but instead, he cried out, "God, if what the Bible says about you is true, I want to see you."

His dad and mom always hoped he would go to seminary to eventually take over the ministry. But Daniel was not ready for that. When he recovered, he decided to go to Jakarta and pursue a career in journalism.

About five years later someone offered him a scholarship to study at a Christian residential journalism training center in Australia. He accepted the offer, and found when he got to Tasmania, that the school was actually a community of twenty-three families with nearly as many young people. He presumed he would be the most pitiable member of the group, but soon learned that others there had suffered greater indignities than him.

One young man, who had watched his father beat his mother every day, had contemplated suicide. Another young man was thrown atop a garbage heap when he was three-months old. And a young woman who washed clothes with him suffered from severe pain and chronic illness. Yet all of these had learned to face life with self-esteem and gratitude toward God.

Daniel realized God had already begun to answer his prayer to know him. He quickly concluded that if God could help these less fortunate than he, God could work in his life, too.

Daniel's experience in Tasmania helped him turn the corner. Ten years later and now thirty-four, Daniel is the National Chairman of the Christ Congregational Church of Indonesia founded by his father. He also serves as liaison with Advancing Native Missions.

Yogyakarta Missionary Training Center began in 1993 with sixteen young missionary workers. To date, the school has trained about 480 workers who are now serving the Lord. Some eighty work directly with Paulus, while the other 400 joined other denominations or church groups. Yet even those maintain relationships with Wibowo and his team.

Each of those serving with Paulus has one or more disciples working under him, so the number of workers serving with Paulus is over a hundred. These have planted some two-hundred churches with a combined attendance of ten-thousand. If you count the work of the other four-hundred, the number of churches planted is close to a thousand.

Sri and Paulus are glad for all of this. By God's grace, Paulus, Sri, and their national family of believers continue to live the Christian example before the people of Indonesia. That's missions exemplified.

The story on Daniel came from a 2020 blog by Marlou Barredo.

Appendices

The Old Testament Foundation of Mission

T he doctrine and practice of mission is commonly understood to stem from the New Testament. But we miss a lot if we fail to understand that mission was God's intent from the beginning.

So before we consider more fully the New Testament's impetus for mission, let us first of all see how the call to mission is imbedded in the Old Testament. We will see that throughout its record God is interested in making Himself known not just to the Jews, but to all nations.

One might consider the command God gave to Adam and Eve a form of missionary imperative:

God blessed them and said to them, "Be fruitful and increase in number; fill the earth and subdue it. Rule over the fish in the sea and the birds in the sky and over every living creature that moves on the ground" (Genesis 1:28).

Of course, we know what happened. Cain killed Abel and eventually the human race became so wicked that God wiped them all out with a flood. He started over with Noah and his three sons and their wives, but even that went awry.

Many sought to build cities for their honor, and a united humankind decided to build a tower to heaven upon which they would worship the stars of heaven and the occult. To halt that attempt, God multiplied their languages and scattered them across the face of the earth. Thus the nations were formed.

But God wasn't rejecting the nations. He still had a love for them and wanted to bring them to Himself.

The Abrahamic covenant

The next clear inference of mission is found in the call of Abraham. After God tells Abram to leave his house and go to a place He will show him, He says He will make of him a great nation, "and all peoples on earth will be blessed through you" (Gen. 12:3). This call or covenant was repeated twice more (18:18 and 22:17-18), and confirmed to Isaac (Gen. 26:4) and to Jacob (Gen. 28:12-14). Each time God implied the blessing would go through them to many nations. Genesis ends with the prophecy:

The scepter will not depart from Judah,
nor the ruler's staff from between his feet,
until he to whom it belongs shall come
and the obedience of the nations shall be his.
                    —Genesis 49:10

Mission with Moses

[Rabbinical Judaism dates Moses 1391-1271 BCE; Christian tradition dates him earlier.—Wikipedia]

We don't usually think of the five books of Moses as missionary material, yet the Song of Moses (Exod. 15:1-18) speaks of the Hebrews' deliverance from Egypt affecting the inhabitants of Palestine, the chiefs of Edom, the mighty men of Moab, and the inhabitants of Canaan, and concludes with, "The Lord shall reign for ever and ever."

Theologians and Bible scholars in general state that the laws of Moses set a standard much higher and more compassionate than those of surrounding countries. Moses commands the people to love the foreigners in their midst (Deut. 10:19). If the people obeyed God's righteous commands, He would bless them abundantly, and "then all the peoples on earth will see that you are called by the name of the Lord, and they will fear you" (Deut. 28:10).

The Book of Revelation uniquely picks up this theme when it says,

And they sang the song of God's servant Moses and of the Lamb:

Great and marvelous are your deeds,
Lord God Almighty.
Just and true are your ways,
King of the nations.
Who will not fear you, Lord,
and bring glory to your name?
For you alone are holy.
All nations will come
and worship before you.
                    —Revelation 15:3-4

Mission in Israel's historical books

What are generally called the "historical books" of the Christian Bible—Joshua through 2 Chronicles—contain myriad references to the knowledge of God extending to all nations. For example, when David cut off Goliath's head, he declared, "The whole world will know that there is a God in Israel" (1 Sam. 17:46).

When David brought the ark into the temple, Asaph and the temple singers sang a song recorded both in 1 Chronicles 16 and in Psalm 105 and Psalm 96. They sang in part:

Declare his glory among the nations,
his marvelous deeds among all peoples.
>   —v. 24, cf. Ps. 96:3

And:

Let the heavens rejoice, let the earth be glad;
let them say among the nations, "The Lord reigns!"
>   —v. 31, cf. Ps. 96:10

When King Solomon dedicated the temple, he prayed that when the fame of the Lord reached other lands and foreigners came to worship God at the temple, God would "hear from heaven [and] do whatever the foreigner asks of you." The purpose was "so that all the peoples of the earth may know your name and fear you, as do your own people Israel" (1 Kings 8:41-43. See also 2 Chron. 6:33). Solomon prayed, "that all the peoples of the earth may know that the LORD is God and that there is no other" (v. 60).

This leads us to consider mission in the Psalms.

Mission in the Psalms

The Psalms are rich in mission phraseology. We will mention only a few of the nearly 50 references.

We can't read far before we come to that astounding Messianic Psalm 2 in which God says to His Anointed:

You are my Son;
today I have begotten you.
Ask of me, and I will make the nations your heritage,

and the ends of the earth your possession. (vv. 7-8 —ESV)
David said, "I will praise you, LORD, among the nations."
    —Ps. 18:49
All the ends of the earth
will remember and turn to the Lord,
and all the families of the nations
will bow down before him.
    —Ps. 22:27

He later speaks of "God our Savior, the hope of all the ends of the earth and of the farthest seas" (Ps. 65:5).

Solomon declares, "May...all nations call him blessed! ...may the whole earth be filled with his glory!" (Ps. 72:17, 19 ESV).

The sons of Korah sang, "therefore the nations will praise you for ever and ever" (Ps. 45:17) and, "Be still, and know that I am God; I will be exalted among the nations, I will be exalted in the earth" (46:10), and "Clap your hands, all you nations; shout to God with cries of joy" (47:1).

Mission in Jeremiah

The idea that God created Israel to be a missionary to the nations comes out strongly in the prophets.

For example, God tells Jeremiah,
Before I formed you in the womb I knew you,
before you were born I set you apart;
I appointed you as a prophet to the nations.
    —Jeremiah 1:5

Jeremiah says eventually "all nations will gather in Jerusalem to honor the name of the LORD" (Jer. 3:17).

He says that if Israel repents and puts their detestable idols out of sight and truly confesses the Lord, "then the nations will invoke blessings by him and in him they will boast" (Jer. 4:20). The ultimate purpose of Israel's covenant relationship with God is that the nations will be blessed—echoes of the Abrahamic covenant.

At least two additional passages speak of reaching the nations with the message of the one, true God:

At that time they will call Jerusalem The Throne of the Lord, and all nations will gather in Jerusalem to honor the name of the Lord. No longer will they follow the stubbornness of their evil hearts.

—Jeremiah 3:17

to you the nations will come
from the ends of the earth and say,
"Our ancestors possessed nothing but false gods,
worthless idols that did them no good.

—Jeremiah 16:19

Even though Babylon will get its eventual and deserved judgment, Jeremiah tells the exiles there to "Pray to the Lord for it, because if it [Babylon] prospers, you too will prosper" (Jer. 29:7). "It is the closest you get to love your enemies in the Old Testament," says Dr. Chris Wright, International Director of Langham Partnership International.

Mission in Isaiah

The knowledge of Yahweh was never to be limited to Israel. "Give praise to the LORD, proclaim his name; make known among the nations what he has done, and proclaim that his name is exalted" (Isa. 12:4).

Isaiah presents God as saying, "Turn to me and be saved, all you ends of the earth; for I am God, and there is no other" (Isa. 45:22).

In 19:24f Isaiah predicts Assyria and Egypt will join with Israel in worshiping Him and repeats the theme that He is the God of all nations.

Isaiah in particular speaks of a future "Servant of the LORD," which we know to be the Messiah, Jesus Christ. "He will bring justice to the nations" Isaiah says, and "In his teaching the islands will put their hope" (Isa. 42:1b, 4b).

By myself I have sworn,
my mouth has uttered in all integrity
a word that will not be revoked:
Before Me every knee will bow;
by me every tongue will swear.
   —Isaiah 45:23

Isaiah quotes God as speaking to His "Servant" relative to the tribes in exile by saying:

It is too light a thing that you should be my servant
to raise up the tribes of Jacob
and to bring back the preserved of Israel;
I will make you as a light for the nations,
that my salvation may reach to the end of the earth.
   —Isaiah 49:6 ESV

The NIV in the above passage uses "Gentiles" instead of "nations." Any time you read Gentiles in scripture, understand that it means the nations.

Listen to me, my people;
hear me, my nation:
Instruction will go out from me;
my justice will become a light to the nations.
My righteousness draws near speedily,
my salvation is on the way,
and my arm will bring justice to the nations.
The islands will look to me

and wait in hope for my arm.
　　　　　—Isaiah 51:4-5

Israel is to be the source of the knowledge of God to the nations:

Come, let us go up to the mountain of the LORD...
The law will go out from Zion
the word of the LORD from Jerusalem.
He will judge between the nations
and will settle disputes for many peoples.
They will beat their swords into plowshares
and their spears into pruning hooks
Nation will not lift up sword against nation,
nor will they train for war anymore.
　　　　　—Isaiah 2:3-4

Nations will come to your light,
and kings to the brightness of your dawn.
　　　　　—Isaiah 60:3

Israel will be a missionary by example:
The nations will see your vindication,
and all kings your glory;
　　　　　—Isaiah 62:2

Isaiah says that as part of his everlasting covenant with David, Israel "will summon nations you know not, and nations that do not know you will come running to you" (Isa. 55:5).

And many are familiar with that passage so often read during the season of Advent:

Arise, shine, for your light has come
and the glory of the LORD rises upon you. ...
Nations shall come to your light,
and kings to the brightness of your dawn.
　　　　　—Isaiah 60:1,3

Again, a passage quoted by Paul in Romans 10:20:

I revealed myself to those who did not ask for me,
I was found by those who did not seek me.
To a nation that did not call on my name,
I said, "Here am I, here am I."
                    —Isaiah 65:1

Isaiah concludes by saying, "I…am about to come and gather the people of all nations and languages, and they will come and see my glory. I will set a sign among them, and I will send some of those who survive to the nations—to Tarshish, to the Libyans and Lydians…, to Tubal and Greece, and to the distant islands that have not heard of my fame or seen my glory. They will proclaim my glory among the nations" (Isa. 66:19).

Indeed, it is the fulfillment of how he began his prophesying:

In the last days
The mountain of the LORD's temple
    will be established
as chief among the nations;
It will be raised above the hills,
and all nations will stream to it.
                    —Isaiah 2:2

Other prophets on mission

That last passage in Isaiah is repeated nearly word-for-word by Micah, a contemporary of Isaiah.

In the last days
the mountain of the LORD's temple will be
    established as the highest of the mountains;
it will be exalted above the hills,
    and peoples will stream to it.
Many nations will come and say,

"Come, let us go up to the mountain of the LORD,
to the temple of the God of Jacob.
He will teach us his ways
so that we may walk in his paths."
The law will go out from Zion,
the word of the LORD from Jerusalem.
He will judge between many peoples
and will settle disputes for strong nations far
and wide.
They will beat their swords into plowshares
and their spears into pruning hooks.
Nation will not take up sword against nation,
nor will they train for war anymore.
—Micah 4:1-3

The prophet Ezekiel had many visions from God. He prophesied to the exiled Jews in Babylon "...not for your sake, people of Israel, ...but for the sake of my holy name, which you have profaned among the nations where you have gone. I will show the holiness of my great name, which has been profaned among the nations... Then the nations will know that I am the LORD, declares the Sovereign LORD, when I am proved holy through you before their eyes" (Ezek. 36:22-23).

Daniel similarly prophesied much about the future, which we cannot get into now. In one of those visions he saw "one like a son of man" [Jesus Christ] standing before "the Ancient of Days" [God the Father]. "He [Christ] was given authority, glory and sovereign power; all nations and peoples of every language worshiped him. His dominion is an everlasting dominion that will not pass away, and his kingdom is one that will never be destroyed" (Daniel 7:13-14).

And of course we all know about Jonah, who was commanded by God to go and preach to Nineveh, the capital city of Assyria. He considered Assyrians enemies and heathen. He was not interested in seeing them saved, and so headed in the opposite direction. God caused a tumultuous storm to arise that threatened the ship. Jonah told the sailors it was his fault because he was rebelling against God, and if they would just throw him overboard, everything would be all right.

They threw him overboard, and the sea immediately calmed. Then God sent a "great fish" that swallowed Jonah whole and vomited him up on dry land three days later. This time Jonah obeyed God, preached a simple message of judgment against Nineveh, and much to his chagrin, the people, including the king, actually repented. We should not be like Jonah and resist sharing God's message. Instead we should gladly share it and rejoice when people receive it, repent of their sins, and are saved.

Habakkuk foresees that "the earth will be filled with the knowledge of the glory of the LORD as the waters cover the sea" (Hab. 2:14).

Zechariah also declares that when the LORD comes, "Many nations will be joined with the LORD in that day and will become my people" (Zech. 2:11).

He quotes God as saying, "Many peoples and powerful nations will come to Jerusalem to seek the LORD Almighty and to entreat him" (Zech. 8:22).

The verse after Zechariah prophesies that Christ will come into Jerusalem riding on a donkey says, "He will proclaim peace to the nations. His rule will extend from sea to sea and from the [Euphrates] River to the ends of the earth" (Zech. 9:10).

"The LORD will be king over the whole earth" (Zech. 14:9).

"My name will be great among the nations," God says twice in Malachi 1:11, the last book in the Old Testament.

Thus we see that throughout the Old Testament—from Genesis through the historical books, in the majestic psalms and the major and minor prophets of Israel, God is depicted as having a great desire to make Himself known to all nations. The creation of Israel was merely one step along the way. From it would come the Savior, and the message of the New Testament.

Indeed, anyone who thinks that reaching out to "all nations" is unique to the New Testament obviously hasn't read the Old.

Jesus the Master Missionary

Mission stems directly from the Lord Jesus Christ, His teachings and His commands. In this chapter we will look at the missions directive as found in the Gospels.

Mission in the Life and Ministry of Jesus

As seen in the last chapter, we have a mission-minded God. In the New Testament we see that Jesus is His primary missionary to this earth. The most beloved verse in the Bible says, "For God so loved the world that he gave his only son, that whoever believes in him should not perish, but should have everlasting life" (John 3:16). Jesus, as the author and finisher of our faith (Hebrews 12:2 KJV), is both the model missionary and the chief sender of missionaries.

As we quoted at the beginning of this book, Jesus told the crowd of apostles and believers gathered after his resurrection immediately before He ascended into heaven, "Therefore go and make disciples of all nations, baptizing them in the name of the Father and of the Son and of the Holy Spirit, and teaching them to obey everything I have commanded you. And surely I am with you always, to the very end of the age" (Matthew 28:19-20).

So without doubt, we are emphatically commanded to go and preach the gospel to people of every nation. And "nation" here means an ethnic or linguistic people group rather than a country with political boundaries. At the climax of this age, some of every nation, language and tribe will be represented in the throng around God's throne in heaven (Revelation 7:9).

The parables of Jesus

That God wants to reach out to all nations with the good news of His redemption, forgiveness and eternal life in Christ is readily apparent in the parables Jesus told.

Jesus spoke several parables depicting the nature of the Kingdom of Heaven. He said it is like leaven or yeast that a woman puts in a batch of dough and eventually the whole batch of dough rises (Mat. 13:33), or like a mustard seed that is the tiniest of all seeds, but after being planted grows large enough for birds to make their nests in it (v. 31-32). The idea here is that the kingdom of God doesn't remain local; it expands greatly.

In the Parable of the Good Samaritan (Luke 10:30-37), Jesus tells of a Samaritan who stops to help a man wounded and left to die by robbers. A Jewish priest and a Levite (an expert in the Old Testament) passed him by, not wanting to corrupt their "holiness" with someone who might be "unclean." But a Samaritan, despised by Jews, did not think of himself, but only of the man in need. He took him to an inn and paid the inn-keeper to look after him.

In the Parable of the Lost Sheep (Luke 15:3-7 and Mat. 13:47), Jesus says God rejoices more over the one sinner who repents and returns to the fold than the 99 other "good" sheep that need no repentance. It is clear God is interested in seeking the lost and not just in caring for those already in his household.

In what is often called the Parable of the Prodigal (Rebellious) Son (Luke 15:11-32), Jesus tells of a younger son who asked early for his share of his father's inheritance, and then squanders it on riotous living. After he had spent everything he had and found himself hungry, destitute and without friends, he decided he would go back to his father's farm and ask to be treated just like one of the hired servants. But the father saw him coming, ran out to meet him, threw his arms around him, kissed him, and then ordered the best robe, sandals and a ring be put on him, and the fatted calf butchered and prepared for a feast.

Meanwhile the older son returned from the field and became incensed that his father would throw a celebration for the scoundrel who wasted his father's inheritance. "You've never done anything for me," he complained, "and I've served you faithfully for years."

"You are always with me," the father said, "and everything I have is yours. But we had to celebrate and be glad because this brother of yours was dead and is alive again; he was lost and is found" (v. 31-32).

Parables concerning Israel

Not only are there many parables showing God's desire to see the individual sinner repent and embrace His love, Jesus told other parables warning Israel that if they were not faithful as a nation, the blessings they expected might be given to others.

In the Parable of the Tenants (Matthew 21:33-45) Jesus speaks of a landowner who plants a vineyard and leases it to tenants, expecting income from its vintage. When the time comes to collect his due, he sends servants to collect the funds, but they are abused and sent away shamefully. Eventually he sends his son, thinking they will respect him. But they kill the son, falsely assuming the vineyard will then be theirs.

When Jesus asks the crowd what the landowner will do, they respond, "He will bring those wretches to a wretched end, and he will rent the vineyard to other tenants, who will give him his share of the crop at harvest time" (v.41). "Therefore I tell you," Jesus told the crowd, "that the kingdom of God will be taken away from you and given to a people who will produce its fruit" (v. 43). The chief priests and Pharisees knew Jesus was talking about them (v. 45).

In the Parable of the Banquet (Luke 14:16-24—called Wedding Feast in Matthew 22:2-14) Jesus tells of a wealthy man who invites many guests to a great banquet. But when the banquet was ready, they all made excuses and didn't come. So the householder told the servants, "Go out quickly into the streets and alleys of the town and bring in the poor, the crippled, the blind and the lame" (v. 21). "That has already been done," they replied.

"Then...go out to the roads and country lanes and compel them to come in, so that my house will be full," the householder said. "I tell you, not one of those who were invited will get a taste of my banquet" (v. 24). If those who were first invited do not care to come to God's banquet, God will seek others perhaps less qualified to take their place.

In the Parable of the Ten Minas (Luke 19:11-27) Jesus tells of a prince who went to a far country to be appointed king and then return. After he left, some of his subjects hated him and sent a delegation after him to say, "We don't want this man to be our king" (v. 14). He was made

king, anyway, and when he returned, he said, "Those enemies of mine who did not want me to be king over them—
bring them here and kill them in front of me" (v. 27).

In the parable the prince also gives minas to several
servants and tells them to invest them or work with them
while he is gone. When he returns the first two have
doubled their capital, but the third servant, who hid his
money in the ground, was reprimanded, and his mina
given to the one who had gained much. This surely is
warning that we who have much should use it for His
kingdom, or we may be sorry. A parable of the Ten
Talents (Matthew 25:14-30) teaches the same lesson.

This is not an exhaustive discussion of Jesus'
parables, but it is sufficient to show that if the Jews did
not embrace Him, his blessings would bypass them and
go to others. The same could be said to many—both Jews
and Gentiles—today.

Jesus' actions and deeds

We do not intend to discuss Jesus' entire life and
ministry here, but simply highlight several incidents
that show that He desired to bring all nations into His
kingdom. It is true that Jesus initially said his focus was
on reaching the Jews (Matthew 10:6; 15:24), but there
are plenty of times He extended his mercies to other
nations.

When Jesus went in the vicinity of Tyre, a Gentile
commercial center, a woman from a part of Syria called
Phoenicia, atop what is sometimes called "the fertile
crescent," asked him to heal her daughter.

"Let the children [of Israel] be fed first," he told her;
"for it is not right to take the children's bread and throw
it to the dogs" (Mark 7:27 ESV).

To this seemingly cruel response of Jesus, provoked the woman to reply, "Yes, Lord; yet even the dogs under the table eat the children's crumbs" (v. 28).

Then Jesus responded, "For this statement you may go your way; the demon has left your daughter" (v. 29). We conclude that Jesus' seemingly cruel first reply was needed to elicit a strong faith response from the woman. After that, He was glad to heal the woman's daughter.

When a centurion, a Roman commander, asked Jesus to heal his servant, he stated that all Jesus had to do was speak the word and his servant would be healed. Jesus, amazed at the centurion's faith, said, "Truly, I tell you, with no one in Israel have I found such faith. I tell you, many will come from east and west and recline at table with Abraham, Isaac, and Jacob in the kingdom of heaven, while sons of the kingdom will be thrown into the outer darkness. In that place there will be weeping and gnashing of teeth." He then told the centurion, "Go, let it be done for you as you have believed." The servant was healed that same hour (Mat. 8:5-13).

The apostle John tells of Jesus returning to Cana in Galilee, where he had turned the water into wine. There "a certain royal official" whose son was sick begged Jesus to come and heal his son. After an exchange of words, Jesus said, "Your son will live." When the official got home, he learned his child was healed at the very moment Jesus uttered those words. It is possible the "royal official" was related to Herod Antipas, the son of Herod the Great, the son of a man from Idumea and a daughter of an Arabian sheik. At least it is probable the man was not a pure-blood Jew.

Shortly after this Jesus traveled to the far side of the sea of Galilee, to the country of the Gerasenes (or

Gadarenes). There a demon-possessed man met him. Anticipating that Jesus was going to cast them out, the spirits in him said, "Send us to the pigs; let us enter them," and Jesus did so. After he was healed, the man wanted to go with Jesus, but Jesus told him, "Go home to your friends and tell them how much the Lord has done for you, and how he has had mercy on you." Then Mark says, "He went away and began to proclaim in the Decapolis (the area of ten Gentile cities) how much Jesus had done for him" (Mark 5:1-20 ESV; Matthew 8 depicts the story with two men).

The Decapolis was a collection of ten cities, nine of which were on the eastern side of the Jordan, with seven being in modern-day Jordan. Their Greek and Roman culture set them apart from the surrounding Semitic culture. So here again we see Jesus ministering to Gentiles.

Even though Jesus sometimes seems to have a narrow focus ("I was sent only to the lost sheep of Israel," Matt. 15:24), that was only His first priority, not His ultimate or total mission. He told the disciples, "I have other sheep that are not of this fold. I must bring them also, and they will listen to my voice. So there will be one flock, one shepherd" (John 10:16 ESV).

Shortly after Jesus made his triumphal entry into Jerusalem, he said, "And I, when I am lifted up from the earth, will draw all people to myself" (John 12:32).

In the Upper Room Jesus prayed for His disciples. He also prayed "for those who will believe in me through their message, that all of them may be one" (John 17:20f).

The whole thing comes to a climax when he tells them after He rose from the dead, "Go therefore and make disciples of all nations, baptizing them in the name of the

Father and of the Son and of the Holy Spirit, teaching them to observe all that I have commanded you. And behold, I am with you always, to the end of the age" (Matt. 28:19-20 ESV).

Then, Luke records in Acts that immediately before He was taken up to heaven, Jesus also told his disciples, "You will receive power when the Holy Spirit comes on you; and you will be my witnesses in Jerusalem, and in all Judea and Samaria, and to the ends of the earth" (Acts 1:8).

This takes us to the missionary activity of the apostles in the Acts of the Apostles.

From Pentecost to Paul

T he church was born at Pentecost through the proclamation of Peter, and continued to develop through Paul as well as Peter and other apostles.

Mission illustrated in the Acts of the Apostles

Most Bible scholars consider that the church began on the Day of Pentecost. Peter, filled with the Holy Spirit, preached a message about the death and resurrection of the Lord Jesus Christ, and 3,000 Jewish men were convicted of their sin, repented, confessed the Lord, and were baptized (Acts 2).

At this point, the focus was on Peter and his actions. He healed a lame beggar on the way to the temple and preached to the multitude who witnessed the miracle, bringing the number of men who believed to 5,000 (Acts 3 and 4).

Stephen strongly contended with the Jews and to silence his voice, the unbelieving Jews stoned him to death (Acts 7).

"On that day a great persecution broke out against the church in Jerusalem, and all except the apostles were scattered throughout Judea and Samaria" (Acts 8:1). Many of them went to the crossroads city in Syria called Antioch on the Orontes River, at that time the third-largest city in the Roman Empire after Alexandria and

Rome. Today the modern city of Antakya-Hatay lies just inside the Turkish border from Syria.

Note two things: First of all, many of the Jews who had come to Jerusalem to celebrate the Feast of Pentecost became believers on the Day of Pentecost. They now returned to the areas from which they had come. That is, they went back to spread the good news about Jesus among their home communities. So they became the first missionaries.

Secondly, the apostles, who we normally think were the first missionaries, actually remained in Jerusalem— at least for a season.

About this same time Philip, one of the seven deacons appointed in Acts 6, went down to a city in Samaria (a region despised by the Jews, composed of half-breeds—people settled there by Nebuchadnezzar who then intermarried with the local population). He preached the gospel among them with astound-ding results: "For with shrieks, impure spirits came out of many, and many who were paralyzed or lame were healed" (Acts 8:7).

In fact, a sorcerer named Simon thought he could buy this power from Philip. Philip rebuked him, and the sorcerer appeared to repent and asked for prayer.

Immediately after this Philip was instructed by an angel to go down to the road that led from Jerusalem to Gaza. There he found a eunuch who was the treasurer of Queen Candace, queen of the Ethiopians. He was probably an Ethiopian Jew, since he was reading the scroll of the prophet Isaiah as he rode in a chariot. Philip asked him if he understood what he was reading, and the eunuch said, "No, how can I, unless someone explains it to me?" (Acts 8:31).

The eunuch was reading chapter 53 describing the cruel and torturous death of the Messiah. Philip told him it referred to Jesus. The eunuch believed in the Lord and was baptized. This no doubt is how the gospel was carried to Ethiopia, probably the first country in Africa to embrace the gospel.

After this, Philip was snatched away by the Spirit and transported to Azotus (another name for the Philistine city of Ashdod). He preached the gospel in many of the towns in that region, ending up in Caesarea on the coast of the Mediterranean (Acts 8:40).

A short time after this, while the apostle Peter was praying on a rooftop while waiting for dinner to be prepared, he saw three times in a vision a sheet full of unclean animals descending toward him. He heard a voice saying, "Get up, Peter, kill and eat" (Acts 10:13). This puzzled Peter because he had never eaten anything "unclean" in his life, and he told the Lord so. The voice replied, "Do not call anything impure that God has made clean" (v. 15).

As soon as the threefold vision vanished, three men came knocking on the door of the house where Peter was staying, asking for him. They told Peter they were sent by a Roman Centurion named Cornelius, who had been bidden in a vision to send for him to come and deliver a message by which he and his household would be saved.

Peter went with the men, and when they arrived at Cornelius' house, he found the place filled with people waiting to hear Peter's message. So Peter preached about Jesus, and as soon as they heard that they could know the forgiveness of their sins by trusting in Jesus, they believed. They were instantly filled with the Holy Spirit as a sign of God's acceptance of them (Acts 10:43-46).

Peter immediately concluded he should baptize them, because they "received the Holy Spirit just as we have" (Acts. 10:47). When Peter shared what happened with the elders in Jerusalem, they concluded, "So then, even to Gentiles God has granted repentance that leads to life" (Acts 11:18).

The baptism and consequent acceptance into the body of Christ of these Romans showed that "Gentiles" or non-Jews could be accepted into the body of Christ without first going through the ritual of becoming Jews. This became a milestone in church history, and was remembered when the apostle Paul explained his ministry among the Gentiles in Acts 15.

Missionary journeys of Paul

When Stephen was stoned (Acts 9), the stone throwers laid their garments at the feet of a young man named Saul. Saul was a young and very zealous Pharisee who had become a great persecutor of the young church. He fervently searched for those who believed in Jesus as their Savior, and had them brought before the Jewish Council for judgment, sometimes even being sentenced to death. Saul had subsequently obtained special papers from the Council to go to Damascus to search for Jesus believers there.

On the way he suddenly fell off his horse, saw a brilliant light, and heard a voice, saying, "Saul, Saul, why do you persecute me?"

"Who are you, Lord," Saul asked.

"I am Jesus, whom you are persecuting," the voice replied (Acts 9:4-5).

Saul was stricken blind and had to be led by the hand. Jesus told him to go to Damascus and there he would be told what to do. After he arrived in Damascus, God, through a vision, instructed a man named Ananias to go and lay hands on Saul, baptize him, and he would recover his sight.

Ananias came and prayed for Saul. Immediately, something like scales fell from Saul's eyes, restoring his sight. He was filled with the Holy Spirit and baptized. After spending several days with the believers in Damascus, Saul, who was a learned Pharisee, began proclaiming Christ as the Messiah in the synagogues of the area.

When Saul learned that some of the Jews wanted to kill him, his friends let him down over the wall of the city in a basket. According to Acts, Saul visited Jerusalem, but when he learned that Jews there also were plotting to kill him, he returned to his home town of Tarsus in Cilicia, which today is the modern city of Mersin in Turkey.

Now those who had been scattered by the persecution that broke out when Stephen was killed traveled as far as Phoenicia, Cyprus and Antioch, spreading the word only among Jews. Some of them, however, men from Cyprus and Cyrene, went to Antioch and began to speak to Greeks also, telling them the good news about the Lord Jesus. The Lord's hand was with them, and a great number of people believed and turned to the Lord.

News of this reached the church in Jerusalem, and they sent Barnabas to Antioch. When he arrived and saw what the grace of God had done, he was glad and encouraged them all to remain true to the Lord with all their hearts. He was a good man, full of the Holy Spirit and faith, and a great number of people were brought to the Lord.

113

Then Barnabas went to Tarsus to look for Saul, and when he found him, he brought him to Antioch. So for a whole year Barnabas and Saul met with the church and taught great numbers of people. The disciples were called Christians first at Antioch.

—Acts 11:19-27

Soon after this the church in Antioch commissioned Barnabas and Saul to go out as missionaries (Acts 13). They went first to the island of Cyprus, Barnabas' homeland, and then traveled to Pisidian Antioch (not to be confused with the Antioch of Syria), about a half-mile north of the modern Turkish city of Yalvaç. During this journey Saul changed his name from the Semitic Saul to the more culturally relevant Paul.

It was Paul's custom to go first to the Jewish synagogue to preach. He had a saying, "to the Jew first, and also to the Greek/Gentile [other nations]" (Romans 1:16). When the Jews objected to Paul's message, Paul said, "Since you reject it and do not consider yourselves worthy of eternal life, we now turn to the Gentiles. For this is what the Lord has commanded us:

"'I have made you a light for the Gentiles,

that you may bring salvation to the ends of the earth.'"

Acts continues, "When the Gentiles heard this, they were glad and honored the word of the Lord; and all who were appointed for eternal life believed" (Acts 13:46-48).

After this, they left Pisidian Antioch and preached the gospel in a number of other cities in Pamphilia, which today is part of southern Turkey. They eventually returned and shared with the church in Antioch of Syria all that had happened (Acts 14:26-28).

At one point Paul visited the esteemed Christian leaders in Jerusalem. "They recognized that [Paul] had been entrusted with the task of preaching the gospel to the uncircumcised, just as Peter had been to the circumcised" (Galatians 2:7).

After returning to Antioch he decided to go again to Pamphilia and see how the churches were faring. This time he kept going west, and at Troas, on the Aegean seacoast, he had a vision of a man of Macedonia, saying, "Come over to Macedonia and help us" (Acts 16:9). Paul and his companions decided to go to Macedonia, the region north of Greece, and thus the gospel entered southern Europe.

Paul visited several cities in Greece, including Philippi and Thessalonica. He dialoged with the philosophers on Mars Hill in Athens, and spent considerable time in Corinth. From there he sailed across the Aegean sea to Ephesus. He then visited several cities in Macedonia again before returning to Troas and from there to Jerusalem, with brief stops along the way at Miletus (where he bid farewell to the elders from Ephesus), Tyre and Caesarea, before taking his overland journey to Jerusalem.

In 2017 I took a tour "Following the Footsteps of the Apostle Paul" led by Dr. Carl Rasmussen of Bethel University in Minnesota. I had presumed that Christianity made its biggest impact among the working classes of people. But when we got to Ephesus, I saw that the "houses on the terrace" were spacious and most had elaborate mosaic floors. I concluded that it would not be hard for a church group of considerable size to gather in the house of such a homeowner, e.g. Lydia in Philippi (Acts 16:40), Titius Justus (Acts 18:17), Aquila and Priscilla (1 Cor. 16:3-5, 15), Nympha (Col. 4:15), Onesiphorus (2 Tim. 1:16; 4:19).

One of Paul's co-workers was a man named Erastus, whom he sent to Macedonia with Timothy (Acts 19:22). Modern translations say that he was "the city's director of public works," while older translations call him "treasurer" (Rom. 16:23). When we got to Corinth, we found a stone uncovered in 1929 engraved in Latin, saying, "Erastus...paved [this road] at his own expense." So it seems the message of Christ was gladly received by the intelligent, educated, and prosperous upper middle class, as well as by laborers and merchants—and mostly in the cities.

While at Jerusalem, Paul was encouraged to worship in the temple to reaffirm his Jewishness, since some Jewish believers thought he might have denied the Jewish religion, since he had spent most of his life preaching to the Gentiles. While in the temple, some non-Christian Jews falsely accused him of profaning the temple by bringing in Greeks who had accompanied him to Jerusalem. An uproar followed and Paul was taken into custody by Roman authorities (Acts 21:17-40). To protect Paul from a Jewish assassination plot, Paul was scurried away to Caesarea. Chapters 22 through 26 of Acts deal with Paul's defense before various authorities.

Paul continued to be held in Caesarea by Governor Felix for more than two years. When Festus, a newly appointed governor, suggested Paul should return to Jerusalem for trial, Paul appealed to Caesar. So he was put on a ship in the custody of a centurion. The ship ran aground in a storm and was wrecked, and all on board spent the winter in Malta. Three months later they sailed again for Rome, and the book of Acts ends with Paul under house arrest in Rome, preaching the gospel to all who would come and hear him.

Missionary teachings of Paul

We have already seen that Paul felt obligated to preach the gospel to the Jew first, but then also to other ethnic people groups—the people of what today is Syria, Turkey, Macedonia, Greece, Rome, etc. Since Greek was the language of the market-place in all these places, having grown up in a Roman city, he had no difficulty speaking the Greek language, the *lingua franca* of their day.

Paul's strategy was to proclaim the gospel where it had not been preached (Romans 15:20). In this vein he wrote to the Romans from Greece, "there is no more place for me to work in these regions" (v. 23)—not because everyone was converted (far from it), but because the gospel had been introduced in that region and vibrant congregations, people who bore the testimony of Jesus Christ, existed.

So what was his compulsion? In 2 Cor. 5:14 Paul says, "For Christ's love compels us, because we are convinced that one died for all, and therefore all died." Paul said he did not preach voluntarily: He was compelled (commanded) to preach by God (1 Cor. 9:16); he had no choice. Therefore, he voluntarily preached without pay; he supported himself.

Paul knew that "everyone who calls on the name of the Lord will be saved" (Rom. 10:13).

But, he continues, "How, then, can they call on the one they have not believed in? And how can they believe in the one of whom they have not heard? And how can they hear without someone preaching to them? And how can anyone preach unless they are sent?" (Rom. 10:13-15a).

Paul said his preaching was "not with wise and persuasive words, but with a demonstration of the Spirit's power, so that your faith might not rest on human wisdom, but on God's power" (1 Cor. 2:4-5).

In fact, though he had many credentials as a Pharisee, he gave that all up for "the surpassing worth of knowing Christ Jesus my Lord" (Phil. 3:5-8). He didn't consider himself perfect, but "forgetting what is behind and straining toward what is ahead, I press on toward the goal to win the prize for which God has called me heavenward in Christ Jesus" (vv. 13-14).

He urged believers to follow his example, and pointed them preeminently to the model of Jesus Christ, "Who, being in very nature God, did not consider equality with God something to be used to his own advantage; rather, he made himself nothing by taking the very nature of a servant, being made in human likeness. And being found in appearance as a man, he humbled himself by becoming obedient to death—even death on a cross! (Phil. 2:6-8).

Paul insisted that no other gospel besides the one he preached should be preached (Galatians 1:6-12), which was that Christ died for our sins and was raised on the third day (1 Corinthians 15:1-8). Therefore Christ fully satisfied the com-mands of the law, freeing us from ritualistic requirements if we but trust only in Christ for our salvation. He claimed that those who believed were the true descendants of Abraham, not those who kept Jewish rituals (Romans 4:11 and 9:8).

We have been saved "by grace...through faith" he told the Ephesians (2:8). He warned the church in Colossae, "See to it that no one takes you captive through hollow and deceptive philosophy, which depends on human tradition and the elemental spiritual forces of this world rather than on Christ" (Colossians 2:8). Therefore they needed not pay attention to rules about eating or drinking special foods or observing special days (2:16-23).

Paul continually quoted the Old Testament to justify his missionary activities (indeed, there wasn't a New Testament yet):

I was found by those who did not seek me;
I revealed myself to those who did not ask for me.
—Romans 10:20 (see Isaiah 65:1)

For I tell you that Christ has become a servant of the Jews on behalf of God's truth, so that the promises made to the patriarchs might be confirmed and, moreover, that the Gentiles might glorify God for his mercy. As it is written:

"Therefore I will praise you among the Gentiles;

I will sing the praises of your name" [see 2 Sam. 22;50; Ps. 18:49].

Again, it says,

"Rejoice, you Gentiles, with his people" [see Deut. 32:43; Isa. 66:10].

And again,

"Praise the LORD, all you Gentiles;

let all the peoples extol him" [see Ps. 117:1].

And again, Isaiah says,

"The Root of Jesse will spring up,

one who will arise to rule over the nations;

in him the Gentiles will hope" [see Isa. 11:10].

"May the God of hope fill you with all joy and peace as you trust in him, so that you may overflow with hope by the power of the Holy Spirit."
—Romans 15:8-13

Paul's goal was that "at the name of Jesus every knee should bow, in heaven and on earth and under the earth, and

119

every tongue confess that Jesus Christ is Lord, to the glory of God the Father" (Philippians 2:10-11 ESV).

So we conclude that the missionary message of the New Testament fulfills the prophecies of the Old Testament about taking the gospel to other nations. It also gives us vital impulse to continue—even complete—the work of mission.

The Apostolic Wave Continues

T he apostolic age generally consists of activities of the original apostles up until their deaths. The only death of an apostle mentioned in the New Testament is that of **James**, the brother of John, who was executed with the sword on Herod's order (Acts 12:2).

Church fathers say that the Roman soldier who guarded James was so impressed with his testimony that he also trusted in Christ and was beheaded along with James.

Tradition says **Mark** accompanied Peter to Rome where he wrote the Gospel of Mark from Peter's remembrances around A.D. 60. After Peter's death he went to Alexandria and planted a church. History confirms his presence in North Africa. One report says he was later dragged by horses until dead. Another legend says he was led through the streets like an animal with a rope around his neck. When he collapsed, he was thrown into a stone prison where he died. But his enemies made ready to burn his body. When they lit the bonfire, a mammoth thunder-clap shook the earth and hailstones fell from heaven smothering the fire. Believers then buried his body peacefully.

Peter was crucified under Nero. He said he was not worthy to die the same way as Christ, and asked to be crucified upside down.

Paul told the Romans he would stop and visit them on his way to Spain (Rom. 15:24,28). Clement of Rome in the late first century and later church fathers said he actually preached there. At the same time Paul wrote the Romans he had already preached the gospel "from Jerusalem all the way around to Illyricum" (v. 19), an area now occupied by Albania, Croatia and Bosnia-Herzegovina.

Back in Rome he was summarily killed with a sword on order of Nero around A.D. 67. It would have been illegal to crucify him, a Roman citizen. Ironically, Nero committed suicide a few weeks later.

What happened to the other apostles?

Matthew, the tax collector, wrote the Gospel of Matthew some 20 years after the crucifixion of Christ and went as a missionary to the Persians, Parthians and Medes. Yet legend says he was martyred in Ethiopia.

Luke, the writer of both the Gospel of Luke and the Acts of the Apostles, was hanged on an olive tree in Greece because of his powerful preaching.

Andrew is reported to have preached the gospel in Cappadocia, Galatia, and Bithynia, ending up in Scythia, Greece, and Achaia, where he was crucified by order of the governor in Patrae. He was tied on a cross in the form of an X, and continued to preach from the cross for two days until he died.

Bartholomew, also known as **Nathaniel**, went as a missionary to present-day Turkey, and was whipped and flayed to death for preaching the gospel in Armenia.

Traditions vary about **Thomas**. Earlier traditions say he went to Persia. Later traditions say he met king Gundaphar who ruled the Indo-Parthian empire of India AD 19-46 who was in Jerusalem seeking a carpenter to build a palace for him. Thomas submitted himself to his employ, went back to India with him, and was empowered to preach the gospel. Many heard the gospel, though some considered his words a threat to their local gods. Eventually they him through with a spear and killed him. Indian Christians today can point to a place outside Chennai (formerly Madras) where he is buried. The Church of St. Thomas, populous in the state Kerala in India, considers him their founding father.

James, the son of Alpheus, was thrown from a 100-foot high pinnacle of the temple. When he survived the fall, his tormentors stoned him and beat his brains out with a club.

Jude, a brother of Jesus, was killed with arrows when he refused to deny his faith in Christ.

Judas, also called **Thaddeus**, took the gospel to Armenia, Syria and Persia, where he was killed with arrows. Another tradition says he was beaten to death with sticks. He is buried in Kara Kalisa in what is now Iran.

Philip preached the gospel in Phrygia and died at Hierapolis near present-day Anatolia in Turkey after being scourged, imprisoned and then crucified in A.D. 54. A tomb believed to be that of the apostle was discovered in Heierapolis in 2012. I visited it in 2017.

Little is certain about **Simon the Zealot** also called Simon the Canaanite. One tradition says he preached the gospel across North Africa, went to Carthage, and then to Spain and ultimately to the British Isles. Legend says he later went to Mesopotamia, and was sawn in two A.D. 70-74.

Matthias, the apostle chosen to replace Judas Iscariot, was stoned by Jews in Jerusalem and then beheaded, although records are sketchy. Another tradition says he preached the gospel in Ethiopia and died and was buried at Sebastopolis.

Barnabas, Paul's companion on his first journey, continued to preach the gospel in Cyprus, his homeland, and in Italy. Legend says he was stoned to death at Salonica.

Eusebius, bishop of Caesarea in Palestine about A.D. 314, was the first person to write the history of the church in the first three centuries in a book. In his ten-volume Ecclesiastical History he wrote:

*Meanwhile the holy apostles and disciples of our Saviour were dispersed throughout the world. Parthia, according to tradition, was allotted to Thomas as his field of labor, Scythia to Andrew, and Asia to **John**, who, after he had lived some time there, died at Ephesus.*

***Peter** appears to have preached in Pontus, Galatia, Bithynia, Cappadocia, and Asia to the Jews of the dispersion. And at last, having come to Rome, he was crucified head-downwards; for he had requested that he might suffer in this way. What do we need to say concerning Paul, who preached the Gospel of Christ from Jerusalem to Illyricum, and afterwards suffered martyrdom in Rome under Nero?*

—Book 3, chapter 1: "The Parts of the World in which the apostles preached Christ" [emphasis added]

Indeed, by the time of the passing of the first generation of apostles, the gospel had been preached throughout the whole Mediterranean world and even as far east as India and as far west as the British Isles.

The sub-apostolic age

Even though the last apostle (John) did not die till around A.D. 95, the apostolic age can generally be considered to have ended in A.D. 70—about 40 years after the ascension of Christ. What makes this demarcation?

Two major events: First is the already-mentioned deaths of the two most prominent apostles, Peter and Paul in A.D. 65-68. The second is the destruction of Jerusalem in A.D. 70 with the center of Christian activity moving to Antioch of Syria and points west.

The Roman General Vespasian was ready to attack Jerusalem when Nero died, and he returned to Rome to be crowned emperor. He then sent Titus to attack Jerusalem in A.D. 70.

Eusebius says that Christians living in Jerusalem at that time received a divine revelation of the impending doom and evacuated the city before the attack. Titus destroyed the city and the temple, leaving only that portion that today is known as the "wailing wall" or "Western wall."

Any surviving Jews—including those believing in Jesus—were without a home, and they scattered. Many ended up in Antioch of Syria, which became the center of Christian activity for the next generation or longer.

Ironically, James' brother, John, is the only one of the original 12 apostles to die a natural death. He eventually traveled to what is Turkey today, became bishop of Ephesus, and was eventually exiled to the Isle of Patmos, where he wrote down the vision that is now the Book of Revelation. I visited his cave hideaway on Patmos in

2017. Even when he was too feeble to walk, legend says he was carried to the church meetings where from a cot he would tell the congregation, "Little children, love one another." He died around the end of the first century.

Spread of the gospel to Africa

As mentioned above, Mark played a major role in taking the gospel to northern Africa, where he eventually met a martyr's death. However, presumably the first man from Africa specifically mentioned to receive the gospel is the Ethiopian eunuch, who was a court official of Candace, Queen of Ethiopia (Acts 8:26-39). Philip, one of the seven deacons appointed by the church in Jerusalem (Acts 6:1-6) was prompted by the Spirit to take the road that ran from Jerusalem to Gaza. There he met a eunuch reading from what we know today as Isaiah 53, and asked Philip to interpret it. This led to the eunuch's conversion and baptism, after which he went on his way rejoicing.

Ethiopia was therefore one of the earliest countries in Africa to receive the gospel, where it was declared the official religion of the state in A.D. 330. It continued as a Christian nation, even after the influx of the Islamic invasion in the 7th century, under the rule of a series of emperors, some claiming descent from King Solomon of Biblical fame and Makeda, the Queen of Sheba, and who bore the title "King of Kings." The authenticity of Solomonic lineage is unproven. The most recent Christian emperor was the famed Haile Selassie who ruled until 1974, when a Communist coup put an end to the emperorship.

Of course, we should note that some of the visitors at Jerusalem on the Day of Pentecost were from "Egypt and the parts of Libya belonging to Cyrene" (Acts 2:10). So it is reason-able to think that they carried the gospel back to Africa after the visitors-now-believers were dispersed in the persecution following the stoning of Stephen (Acts 8:4). One of the most ancient branches of Christianity today are the Copts of Egypt, who comprised the majority religious group there from the fourth century until the Muslim conquest in the early seventh century.

During the first few hundred years, Alexandria in Egypt became a stronghold of the Christian faith. One of the more famous church fathers from Africa was Augustine (A.D. 354-430), Bishop of Hippo, a city of Egypt. When the Western Roman Empire began to disintegrate, Augustine described the church as the City of God in the book by the same title, and was highly thought of by the later Protestant Reformers.

Spread of the Gospel in Asia and Europe

Meanwhile, Christians still suffered persecution under Roman Caesars up until around A.D. 300. In 312 Constantine the Great saw a vision of the cross in the sky with these words, *in hoc signo vinces* ("in this sign conquer"). He painted crosses (in the form of an "X") on the shields of his soldiers, and defeated his rival, Maxentius, in the Battle of Milvian Bridge. In 313 Constantine met with Licinius in Milan where they agreed to grant Christians freedom to practice their religion, and restore all properties confiscated from the Christians. This is some-times called the Edict of Milan, though no copy of an official "edict" has been found. Licinius had control of the Eastern provinces, while Constantine controlled Rome and Europe.

Constantine himself became an official Christian and was baptized on his death bed. The thought at that time was that the closer to death one was baptized, the fewer sins one would commit after baptism, and thus the less hindrance one would have of entering heaven.

About the Author

J ohn Lindner pastored churches in Michigan and Ohio for 17 years before answering God's call to serve native missions. He moved his family to Charlottesville, VA in 1979 and assumed the first of three positions he would hold over the next 38 years as magazine editor for organizations focusing on native missions, the most recent being Advancing Native Missions.

During these years he wrote *God's Special Agents*, telling the remarkable stories of a dozen indigenous mission leaders from around the world; *The Mountains Shall Sing*, the biography and work of pioneer missionary P. M. Thomas in Kashmir, India; and co-wrote *My Hundred-Year Missionary Adventure* about the life of William Hopper.

John holds a BA from Elmhurst College and a BD from Lancaster Theological Seminary, along with an honorary Doctor of Mission degree from the Evangelical Theological Seminary in Kota, Rajasthan. He is also a lifetime member of the Evangelical Press Association.

John continues his writing and editing services in Charlottesville, VA., as he holds dear the memory of Jo Ann, his beloved wife of 56 years, and takes joy in the time he spends with their four children, their spouses and six grandchildren.

Advancing Native Missions

J esus made a promise in Matthew 24:14 — "This gospel of the kingdom will be preached among all nations." At ANM, we cherish that promise, and we believe that every Christian has a part to play in that mission.

That's why since 1992 ANM has helped Christians and local churches get involved in global missions in ways that make sense for them. Donations to ANM support native Christian workers sharing the gospel among the least reached people of the world. These workers are already accustomed to the languages, cultures, and living standards where they live, so donors can accomplish more with less while participating in the global body of Christ.

We will keep sharing the Good News together until all people everywhere will hear the story of Jesus.

To learn more, visit advancingnativemissions.com.